MOSAIC

MOSAIC
From BROKENNESS
to GOD'S MASTERPIECE

MARJORIE SCHAEFFER

XULON PRESS

Xulon Press
2301 Lucien Way #415
Maitland, FL 32751
407.339.4217
www.xulonpress.com

Printed in the United States of America

Paperback ISBN-13: 978-1-6628-1672-7
Ebook ISBN-13: 978-1-6628-1673-4

TABLE OF CONTENTS

Dedication   vii
Preface   v
Chapter 1. My Damascus Road   1
Chapter 2. Reflections   15
Chapter 3. Now What?   21
Chapter 4. Transition   33
Chapter 5. Divine Opportunity   44
Chapter 6. England Assignment   56
Chapter 7. His Secret Dwelling Place   75
Chapter 8. I'm A Designer!   86
Chapter 9. My Sifting   115
Chapter 10. His Word Is Life!   129
Chapter 11. Restoration   144
Chapter 12. Doors Closing   161
Chapter 13. Florida Here We Come!   177
Chapter 14. A Door Opens   186
Chapter 15. Life In Pittsburgh   199
Chapter 16. Surgery & More   216
Chapter 17. Keys For A Victorious Life   236
Daily Personal Devotions   253
Becoming A Child of God   256
Quotations, Reproducting Material and Disclaimer   257

DEDICATION

I dedicate this book to my three adult children and my three grandchildren, without whom there would have been no story. You have taught me how to love!

To Aria, my only daughter; you'll never know how much you have taught me! Your accomplishments inspire the entire family. I smile when I remember the hilarious fun we had together on those infamous cruises! And your post-surgery care for me demonstrated what a fine physician and care-giver you are! To your Konnor: I shall never forget your accompanying me to the auto train when I moved to Pittsburgh. That so exemplified your frequent kindness to me.

To Tim, my sandwiched-in-the-middle-child, just like me. From infancy onward you always were the proverbial butterfly evading the catcher's net; a free spirit! You have been a trail blazer and your leadership has become a cohesive factor in our family. You exude generosity!

To my beautiful grand-daughter, Jeni: my life has been enhanced by the memories we have shared in Thailand and here when you came for a visit...the game of 'Mimi, May I?', bedtime stories of 'Bear' and cooking classes together in Thailand!!

To my son David, your faith is a rock. The art and music you create inspire angels. I shall forever be grateful for your standing by me in the darkest of times. Oh! The crazy laughter you have brought me...the goofy raisin-man dance you would perform behind the scenes while

I was trying to lecture to my design students! And being there when I took my fall! To your lovely Juju whom God picked out just for you; she has been like a daughter to me.

To the boys, my talented grandsons Zyon and Timmy; the fond memories I have of them would fill a book! Zyon, our games of make-believe and tales of *'Water Commissioner'* will forever make me smile! Timmy, my standing- on- a- kitchen- chair baking partner; I shall always remember the problems we solved on our many *'chats on the stairs'*.

And to all my many wonderful friends: There are too many to list, but each of you has enhanced my life beyond words! Pastor Ken Hughee, being your Vangaurd team as well as standing in the gap for you and your ministry has been and continues to be such an honor and joy. Thank you all for your love and friendship!

To God be the glory for writing my story and inspiring me to share it with my Readers! He has been my Rock, my Guide, my comfort and heartbeat! He has never let me down!

PREFACE

This is my story; the story of one ordinary woman's victory over life's challenges through the grace and love of an extraordinary God. This is not so much a story of my faith, but more importantly of God's amazing faithfulness to me. I am hopeful that my story will encourage readers to have hope in the midst of their own life struggles. He has used the broken dreams and disappointments of my life to perfect His strength through my weakness. In me, *"God has chosen the weak things of this world to shame the strong"* (1 Cor. 1:27).

As He required things of me which were beyond my ability, talents or training, mysteriously I became just the vessel through which He could work. He was the Potter and I became the Clay. Together we would partner to get the job done.

I have faltered, failed and made mistakes, but He has always been there to pick me up and encourage me. Disappointments, misunderstandings and injustices have been my schoolmaster. His Word says that, *"He has put my tears in His bottle"* (Ps. 56:8 KJV). Not one tear has fallen to the ground without His knowledge and deep compassion. He used my struggles to teach me to cling to Him for comfort while encouraging me with hope and faith to go on.

There were seasons of achievement and refreshment. But it was in those night seasons that my comfortable support systems of reasoning, natural strength and intellect were darkened so that my only resource was to learn to walk by faith! He was just waiting for me in those dark, bittersweet ditches to teach me life's greatest lessons!

He replaced my fear with faith; my impatience with His patience, my need with His provision and my desperation with His hope. He gave me endurance in exchange for deep, dark valley experiences. I painfully learned to submit and surrender to Him when it went against my own strong will. I have waited, waited and waited upon the Lord only for Him to renew my strength rather than provide the instant gratification my impatient nature so desired. I slowly came to realize that in His wisdom He had given me the better gift. He has proven to me again and again that, *"His strength will equal my days"* (Deut. 33:25).

He kept His word to me that He would *"never leave me nor forsake me"* (Deut. 31:8). And my shattered broken life was put together again like a piece of mosaic art; one restored piece at a time. Eventually, as if through osmosis, my old fears, anxieties and sorrows mysteriously became courage, confidence and strength. Just as a mosaic art piece must endure fire to become the perfected piece of art its designer intended, so my potential is being realized through the crucible of suffering in the Refiner's white hot flame. I am becoming His Masterpiece.

Through it all, the *"Joy of the Lord has been my (constant) strength"* (Neh. 8:10). How wondrous!

CHAPTER 1

MY DAMASCUS ROAD

THERE THEY GO!
In the silence of the empty driveway, with gut-wrenching sobs contorting my body and the fumes of his car's exhaust still in my nostrils, those quiet words the Lord Himself whispered to me a few years earlier now echoed loudly in my ears,

"Have you counted the cost?"

That day was undoubtedly the most dreadful day of my life, the day in which my fondest dreams were shattered into countless tiny pieces like grains of sand. My very purpose for living had just driven down the driveway to build a new life... WITHOUT me!!!

The image of the old, familiar station wagon rolling down the drive would haunt me for many years to come. I would remember every detail of the children's last waves good-bye and the confused expressions on their young, innocent faces as they gradually disappeared out of my sight into oblivion. I wouldn't see them again for months and it would be many, many years before the relationships with me and Aria and Tim would be restored.

My heart-ache consumed me! It just ate me up! How could I go on? The arms of despair gripped me so tightly that it felt like life itself was being squeezed out of me! Grief and fear took turns tormenting me as I stood there dumbfounded, wondering how the horror of this dramatic, catastrophic moment had evolved. How could I have been so misunderstood, betrayed and now abandoned by those I loved so deeply?

A destiny of love and marriage and raising a family had been the focus of all my childhood dreams. How had our once idyllic family dissolved? How had I become the ENEMY in my own home?

I painfully relived the steps that led to this very moment.

MY DARLINGS

RELIVING THE STEPS   I grew up in a non-Christian home. My parents were moral, ethical people and provided well for our family materially. But there was no spiritual nourishment. I was born hungry. For God. When I was six years old, in the first grade, I became bed ridden for many months with rheumatic fever. This was a time of isolation for me; a time of being set aside. I believe God earmarked those days to cultivate my capacity for Him. During my illness my sister's friend gave me a book with a chapter about Jesus. Although I had never before heard about Jesus or had ever attended church I began talking to Him. Constantly. I clearly remember my little-girl childish prayers, *"Jesus, would you please heal me so I could get out of bed and go play with my friends?"*

In time He did heal me. Well into my adulthood He even healed me of that lingering heart murmur. He became my constant companion. I was never alone. That back bedroom of our home became my sanctuary. And the joy of the Lord filled me up!

Years later a family friend told me that when he and his wife came to visit my parents he would come into my room to try to cheer me up only to leave the room with tears in his eyes because the room's atmosphere was so charged with the joy of the Holy Spirit! Of course, Jesus was there constantly filling the room with His Light and Life because of the spiritual hunger of a little girl who wanted to know Him. Isn't He just wonderful?

THERE WERE MANY MONTHS OF BEDREST
DURING MY BOUT OF RHEUMATIC FEVER.

HERE I AM AS A LITTLE GIRL

I began to occupy my time by playing "church" as I imagined it to be. I would spend my week preparing for Sunday and the church service I would conduct. Lining my dolls and stuffed animals at the foot of my bed we would worship together. My mother had given me manuscript paper not knowing it was to become my tool for writing hymns and praise music for my weekly 'church meetings'. I would preach a sermon, too. All of this from a little girl who had never been to church or heard the gospel. And my family never knew what I was up to in that quiet sanctuary-room in the back of the house; that God Almighty was carving out a place for Himself in my little-girl heart! I truly believe that the faithful prayers of my grandparents had reached heaven and altered the course of my life. Never doubt the power of prayer!

Throughout my childhood I always wished that my family would talk about God, that we would attend church together, even say a blessing at our mealtimes together. Just as I was about to celebrate my tenth birthday a church flyer detailing the Easter story of resurrection somehow was mailed to our home. When Mom asked me what I wanted for my birthday, my response probably wasn't what she expected from her young daughter. *"For my birthday I would really love, love, love you to read to me the story on that flyer about Jesus!"* That is what I wanted for my birthday. I was a good reader and could have easily read the story myself, but I just wanted to share that with her. My request must have put her on the spot. The embarrassment I realized she felt confused me.

My mother would drive me to the church services my friend's family attended, but to my disappointment never showed any interest in coming in to worship with me.

During my freshman year in high school I was invited to attend a revival meeting in the church where my friend's father was the pastor. The visiting evangelist had been in the Nazi Youth Movement and he shared a powerful testimony of how his conversion to Christianity radically transformed his life of hate into one of love and compassion. A group of us from my school all accepted Christ as our Savior that night in a tear-wrenching altar call of repentance. We were all broken under the burden of our sin as conviction compelled us to confess Jesus as our Savior. It was then that He came into my heart to live. Oh! It was wonderful! I knew that Jesus died for me and that I was saved from my sin. And I was assured of heaven someday! What joy filled my young heart! The seeds of my salvation had been cultivated earlier in my young life, but now I was actually *born again!* That was the real beginning of my Life!

A constant thread being woven throughout my life was spiritual opposition. Worldly values were constantly at war with Godly ones. Those closest to me would pull me away from my deepest spiritual hunger. I longed for my parents to attend my baptism by immersion, but they took no interest. They were especially opposed to me attending the bible church in which I was saved. That church was a small congregation of simple, dedicated but uneducated folk. They had great hopes for their young people as evidenced by their openly praying for each of us by name at the weekly prayer meetings. I know those prayers have chased me down during my life by continually drawing me to God.

One night during a prayer service the peaceful atmosphere created by the Lord's presence was abruptly interrupted by an unexpected disturbance! The doors to the sanctuary were raucously flung open with a bang! There in the threshold of the doorway stood my dad, all 6'3" of him, a dark picture of raging emotions as he vented loudly to the congregation. Cringing next to each other in a front pew, my sister and I were horrified! *"What is he doing here? We are in serious trouble",* we shamefully whispered to each other, shrinking into our pew hoping that he wouldn't discover us.

He began to rant to the entire congregation, *"My daughters are no longer allowed in this place! You bible-bangers!! You will NOT be seeing them again! You people are nothing but fools!"* And then as his eyes eventually located us he commanded my sister and me, *"You girls come home immediately!"*

After that, I was no longer allowed to attend my church or any other evangelical bible-preaching church. As long as I resided under my parent's roof I would attend a more traditional church which they accepted. I wouldn't be nourished with the spiritual food my soul longed for. Although I hungered for a deeper revelation of the Truth, it was not to be at that stage of my young life.

I imagined a future in which I would be happily married and have my own family. I had no aspirations of a career. I had so much love inside of me. I knew I had all the makings to become a role model wife. I could be that Proverbs 31 woman! After all, I was loving and affectionate, creative, industrious and principled. My husband and I would be devoted to one another. Television would not dominate our home, rather ours would be a home filled with good books, nutritious food, art, and music. Laughter would abound. Neighborhood children would opt to congregate there.

My handsome children would be smothered with hugs and kisses, confident that they were loved! They would be the most precocious and gifted of all children; loyal and true to one another. Our Christ-centered family life would be bubbling over with Life and Love!

Perhaps it was an unrealistic dream, but somehow those dreams became a self-fulfilling prophecy for a time. Before I had completed two years of college my Prince Charming swept me off my feet and my fantasy began to unfold. Following a storybook wedding while I was yet in my teens we began to create our own fairy tale life. The children came along. Fulfilling my fantasy they were indeed the most precocious of all; so lovable and the greatest joy of my life! I honestly didn't think that anyone loved their children as much as I. Life was sweet! I was in love with love and living what I believed to be my destiny.

YOUNG FAMILY   We had moved from the Pacific Northwest to Bethlehem, Pennsylvania where my husband had been awarded a Ford Foundation grant to become a Ph. D graduate student. Our life in the beautiful Pennsylvania countryside was full of discoveries as we built a strong family life together. I gladly met the challenge of running a household on the limited income supplied by a meager government graduate student stipend. I stretched the grocery budget by shopping farmer's markets, baking our own bread, reconstituting powdered milk, and clipping coupons. Outlet fabric warehouses provided goods for me to make our clothing, tailor-made slipcovers, and draperies. Christmas decorations and gifts were homemade, with ingenuity being the main ingredient, coupled with recycled materials. It was definitely worth the financial sacrifice to stay at home raising the children rather than work outside the home as did so many other mothers in my circumstances.

I had been reading and re-reading Robert McCloskey's beautifully illustrated, *One Morning in Maine* to the children. His graphic watercolor illustrations eventually enticed us to explore the coast of Maine for ourselves. Truly, New England stole our hearts. I suppose that I had been longing for the majestic coast of Oregon where I had grown up. But, instead of returning to the Pacific Northwest as originally planned my husband accepted a position as an instructor at the University of Maine in Portland.

We piled ourselves and our earthly possessions in the old Chevy carryall, one child in our family than when we had embarked on our adventure, three-month-old Baby David. We scraped pennies together for a down payment on a large, old white elephant Victorian two-family house in an established city neighborhood and began to put down roots in Portland. Bright little six-year-old Aria was at the top of her class in second grade, while curious Timmy was surely the most cunning in his kindergarten class!

The challenges of building his new career were the focus for my husband. Slowly, the demands of my own life began to sap my already frail, post-pregnancy constitution. I was single-handedly trying to make our drafty old house a beautiful environment for our family while juggling the demands of motherhood and homemaking. I spent countless hours scraping layer after layer of old wallpaper from the walls, wire-brushing an endless inventory of antique radiators of their peeling paint, refinishing furniture, and sewing draperies for the entire house. Barn sales, auctions, and second-hand stores slowly supplied the furnishings for our home. I developed quite a nose for a bargain for our home and family, as well as learned how to make my home beautiful on a shoestring! The seeds were being sown for my eventual interior design career! But I am getting way ahead of myself!

STIRRINGS IN MY SPIRIT   I stumbled upon an art show featuring the artists Robert and Frances Hook which moved me to my core. His art portrayed Jesus as a virile, strong compassionate man rather than the emaciated figure so often portrayed by earlier artists, while his wife, Francis, painted the children in his art. The emotion, strength, and love portrayed by the Jesus in those paintings deeply stirred my heart. Although I had received Christ as my Savior, I still had not totally yielded my life to His Lordship. In the process rationalization and doubt had brought me into deception.

My foundational Christian beliefs had begun to be challenged leading me to examine more liberal concepts of Christianity. I became so deceived that I was unable to recognize the depths of my sinfulness. Because I hadn't committed the obvious outward sins, was a *'good girl,'* and lived a wholesome life, I didn't recognize the vileness of my innate sinful nature. It is easier for those who commit *'more obvious sins'* to realize their need for salvation. But the *'good girls'* of this world can become so deceived by their *goodness*!

The scriptures say that *"Our righteous acts are like filthy rags"* (Is. 64:6) compared to His Holiness. *"All have sinned and fall short of the glory of God"* (Rom. 3:23) no matter how good we may consider ourselves. We can be deceived into thinking our good works will earn salvation for us, but the scriptures clearly refute this. Paul wrote, *"By grace you have been saved by faith... not from yourselves, it is the gift of God—not by works, so that no one can boast"* (Eph. 2:8) It is only when we recognize our sinful state, and consequently our need for a Savior, that we can truly repent and take on His righteousness by believing in Him. *"To all who did receive Him, to all who believed in His name, He gave the right to become children of God"* (John 1:12). Although we are all made in His image only those that receive His righteousness instead of their good works are the children of God. Unlike the world's teaching, not everyone is a child of God.

Very subtly I had actually slipped into rationalizing my own sin nature! The devil is a liar frequently using deception as his weapon. Somewhere along the way during those early days in Maine, something was going flat in my life. My usual enthusiasm and zest for life started to sour. Spiritual stirrings were going on, although at the time I perhaps didn't realize to what extent. Although my husband had never made a personal commitment to Christ as I had in my teens when we married he promised he would attend church with me and raise our children in the church. No matter how much of a fairy tale we had created, our foundations were rooted in different kingdoms, a sure formula for eventual conflict.

DAMASCUS ROAD EXPERIENCE   One Sunday morning I walked alone to the nearby neighborhood church we had been attending as a family. It was a beautiful day for a walk so I took the long way home, winding my way through our lovely old tree-laden neighborhood, slowly contemplating my life. How could I have known that what was about to occur would become pivotal moments upon which I would reflect for the remainder of my life? The stirrings in my spirit over the previous months had set the stage for what was about to happen!

As I slowly headed toward home that beautiful morning, the unmistakable, undeniably clear, righteous voice of the Lord God Almighty somehow invaded my senses in such a way that the ears of my human spirit were quickened to distinctively hear what He had to say to me! Yes, I heard the voice of the Lord speak to me without a doubt! I hadn't even been calling out to Him. In fact, at that particular moment, I wasn't even thinking of anything vaguely spiritual! He was thinking of me though and had prepared me for such a time as this. It was my time!

Although His words were inaudible they echoed in my mind for years to come as a reminder of those memorable moments; my own Damascus Road experience! Those few words rocked my world and forever turned me inside out!

It was amazing how such a quiet inner voice could speak so distinctly, so clearly, yet penetrate so deeply. It was His still, small voice...the undeniably still, small holy voice of God; words that would strengthen me beyond measure when the floods came...and indeed the floods did come! There was no questioning it. He captured my full attention! Then He spoke my name. Yes, He called me by name:

"Marjorie...Are you tired of doing things your way?"

Those few words rocked my world! Suddenly a giant laser-floodlight flashed into the innermost depths of my being as He showered my senses with the ugliness of my sinful nature. A crystal clear instant awareness overtook me that living my life in my own strength was the sin of which I was guilty and had been unaware. I was desperately in need of His cleansing. My self-righteousness, pride, and sinful nature in that one instant became deplorable and absolutely repulsive to me.

My shame overwhelmed me!!!

I realized that even my best qualities were motivated and tainted by my own needs and desires.

Even the love I had for my family was rooted in Self... My Self. It was all about My Self. I was desperately despicable! As my shamefulness, desperation, and despair reached its height the Voice again spoke in my spirit:

"Marjorie, My daughter,

... I've been waiting for you,

...Are you ready to surrender to Me now?

Although as a young girl of fourteen I had accepted Jesus as my Savior, in that Divine moment I shamefully realized I hadn't made Him *Lord of my life*. I had hungered for Truth. But, now Truth became a Revelation! What a vast chasm lies between the two!

There was no deliberation. His probing question required my life answer and my hearty response was offered without hesitation! After recognizing the truth of my wretched sinful condition it was the sweetest relief to eagerly and unconditionally surrender: *"Yes, Lord. Oh, yes, yes, yes!"* With a potpourri of tears of gratitude and shame rolling down my cheeks, I again audibly responded...*"A THOUSAND TIMES YES!"*

I was undone! With utter abandonment I gave up! Total surrender! A burden I had not realized I was carrying blew away like a feather. Tsunami liquid waves of love poured over my head and down my body. This was the love I had always longed for; that nothing else had ever satisfied! Oh! The love of God! Even now as I write this many years later, there has never been another moment in my life when I felt so secure, so loved, so safe, and fulfilled. Pure liquid honey-gold love, impossible to define or adequately describe, saturated my entire being as I was drenched in the undeniable, indefinable, ecstatic love of God! In the annuls of heaven that scene must have been recorded to inspire the saints throughout eternity!! I will watch it again one day and be blessed!

Heaven had come down and embraced me with the majestic, overwhelming love of God! This love would carry me through a lifetime, keeping me grounded even when everything around me was crazy unsettled. It didn't matter. The Almighty God, maker of heaven and earth, loved even me! More than I could contain! My life would never be the same!

I remembered seeing a compelling ad in a children's magazine of shoes with coil springs on the soles which would allow the wearer to soar, almost reaching Heaven with every step. My feet were instantly shod with those magical Jumping Jack shoes! Euphoria! I was free. Nothing could bind me now; I had tasted the real thing. I was a *gazelle*! I was an eagle soaring over all of life's mountains. I was free!

In the past, I had longed to share unity in Christ with my husband, but sadly because of his unbelief, I had allowed my relationship with the Lord to be compromised; diluted. I so wanted to go there with him, my life-partner. But now, I was instantly free from those shackles! I would serve Christ whether my husband did or not. He was in the Lord's hands; I was free from the burden of his salvation! It was not my responsibility to save him! I just wanted to love him like I had been loved and was now on a mission to do so! The love of God had freed me from the chains of bondage! I would be the Lord's bond-servant even if no one would go with me!

The ecstasy of that moment was pierced by another sobering quiet question. The question that would haunt me over the years! The question to which I could respond only one way. That poignant question: *"Have you counted the cost?"* demanded my response.

And then came a deafening silence as He patiently waited for my answer. I knew my response was crucial. Although His question startled me, after tasting the powerful, fulfilling love of God there was no choice. I was His, cost or no cost. I was smitten; fully surrendered. My heart had been turned inside out. My burden had been lifted; my soul set free. The love of God had kindled my spirit and I would never be the same.

Throughout my life many times that silent question would roar again in my solitude, "HAVE YOU COUNTED THE COST?"

Anything of value will be costly. My decision would carry a cost, too. *"What did it cost me?"* you ask. It would cost everything dear to me. Although it cost me everything, the cost was nothing compared to the price Jesus paid for me! It was a no-contest.

This was my Damascus Road experience; my baptism of the Holy Spirit! Just as Saul of Tarsus had instantly been transformed from one whose religiosity kept him from recognizing who Jesus was, I, too, was transformed in an instant by the revelation of Christ and my desperate need for Him to be the Lord of my life! Although I had once accepted Jesus as my Savior, He had now and forevermore become my *Lord.* I was filled with the joy of His beautiful life-giving Spirit!

Overflowing with the love of God I bounded up the walkway to our home a radiant new woman! I greeted my husband with a sparkling clean brand new love. It wasn't about his shortcomings any longer or about having my needs met. I kissed and hugged the children, my dearest treasures, with a newly kindled love. I could now love them all with God's love, so much richer than the natural love of a wife and mother!

The days and months passed. I had an insatiable, gnawing hunger for the Word of God. I couldn't get enough of Him! My days were filled with joy erupting out of my most innermost being. I was easily moved to tears by God's spirit. I wanted to serve Him where He had placed me, loving my family with the pure love of God!

Yet I would wonder from time to time what He had meant by, *"Have you counted the cost?"*

It would become apparent.

CHAPTER 2

REFLECTIONS

S PIRIT-FILLED CHURCH   One of the radio broadcasts I found especially encouraging was being aired from Portland, Maine by an upcoming preacher who had his own life-changing Holy Spirit encounter in the backwoods of Maine. His inspirational understanding of the scriptures was incredible! He seemed to have committed most of the Bible to memory! Although his church at that time was an hour's drive up the Maine coast he was teaching weekly Bible studies in Portland. To my delight after hearing some of the radio broadcasts my husband agreed to attend his Bible studies with me. I longed to become a member of that church, but couldn't imagine that my husband would agree to it. I wanted him to be the spiritual leader in our home, even though he was not even a believer yet. I just wanted to honor the divine order of God's design for the marriage relationship. So rather than relentlessly coax him, instead I prayed and trusted that the Lord would direct him to make the decision for us to attend the new church together as a family.

Imagine my joy when he suggested one day that we withdraw from the little traditional neighborhood church we had been attending to become members of that church up the coast!!

The new church was exploding under the power of the Holy Spirit. The Lord was drawing spiritually hungry folks of diverse backgrounds and cultures from all over the country to be part of this movement, our common denominator being our hunger for more of the Lord.

What an incredible experience it was to watch a Bible-college emerge as a result of the fires of this outpouring. Students were radical for Jesus, hungry for the Word, and began voraciously committing the Bible to memory. Biblical principles were not only taught in a very balanced manner, but those truths became our experience! In that atmosphere, there was no room for offense! Every time the congregation gathered there was such a strong presence of the Holy Spirit and the love of God that we were compelled to worship and love one another. It was in this atmosphere that many lives were delivered from bondage and sin. Miraculous healings and signs and wonders occurred every time we assembled. Young people came by the droves and were set free from drugs, alcohol, sin, and the hippie lifestyle. This is what the church should be...alive and vital, led by the Holy Spirit rather than tradition and dead orthodoxy. I felt so blessed to sit under the anointing of this ministry and partake of such a move of God.

The Lord had blessed me with a very godly spiritual mother who attended my church. She was the epitome of a Proverbs 31 woman, someone I admired greatly. She was an elegant, beautiful woman in her mid-fifties, filled with wisdom and Godly counsel which she often shared with me. We spent hours on the phone. She had such compassion for what I was going through and would often pray for me and my family. My church held Sunday evening services which were followed by an informal *after service* of more praise, worship, and prayer. One specific evening there were only a few of us in that second service following a deeply moving message in the earlier service. The praise and worship were thick with the Lord's sweet anointing! Betty was sitting with her husband just a few feet diagonally in front of me. I could almost touch her. I noticed her head had slumped onto her husband's shoulder. As peacefully as a gentle breeze she had just breathed her last breath! Strangely, I was not worried or concerned, but just began praying with total confidence that the Lord would revive her! I did not doubt that we were about to see a miracle! The Word commands us to *"Heal the sick and raise the dead!"* (Matt.10:8). While peacefully seated in my pew the Lord spoke to me, *"You will experience 'Greater things than these because I go to the Father'"* (John 14:12). There was no doubt at all that resurrection was about to occur!

The pastor was alerted. A nurse in the congregation came forward to take Betty's pulse, reporting that she had been without a heartbeat for about twenty minutes! Then, miraculously, as we prayed and watched, Betty's face regained color, from grayish-blue to her usual soft ivory skin tone. She raised her head, rose to her feet, and marched to the podium to belt out the song *Because He Lives* with tremendous vitality and strength! She had been in the Lord's powerful presence. Those of us in the church were overwhelmed; stricken with the awesomeness of the miracle we had just witnessed! A holy hush fell over the congregation; a few of us lingered in the tangible presence of the Lord. Betty and her husband left for the hour-long drive to return home. I was still visibly awestruck when I finally arrived home but did my best to report to my husband what had happened that evening. He thought I had lost my mind!

TWO KINGDOMS   Time passed. The Holy Spirit had been nudging my husband. The Word of God will do its work of convicting the individual being exposed to it. He could see that my life-changing experience of three years earlier and the Holy Spirit's moving in me was producing fruit, but this fruit was not a result of his doing. A spiritual war was prevailing apart from our own flesh and blood. *"We wrestle not against flesh and blood, but against principalities, against powers, against the rulers of the darkness of this world, against spiritual wickedness in high places"* (Eph. 6:12 KJV).

Spiritual tension grew. Where was the wonderful person I had married? He probably asked the same question! The tension in our once peaceful home grew. He stopped attending the church services with me and deeply resented the two weekly services I attended. Two kingdoms were being revealed, darkness and light. Eventually he declared complete rejection of the convicting biblical teaching he had been hearing in our church, rather he professed a bold atheistic stand as he began to sulk and withdraw. Something was going on. The darkness intensified.

Two kingdoms.

THE VACATION   We had planned a four-week family vacation to visit our parents in Seattle alternating weeks with each family. The first week we spent with his family. Early in our visit we decided to take a bicycle ride around Green Lake. When we stopped for a rest the conversation took a twist I never could have predicted, but which explained his pensive withdrawal over the past few weeks. His voice took on that professorial tone, *"I think you should go back to school to become financially secure."*

Those words became a pivotal line in the sand. A turning point indeed! Although I never claimed to be a rocket scientist it was evident where this conversation was going. I was not in the least bit prepared for this. I was horrified!!! I was speechless, unable to process what I was hearing. What could lie ahead for me?

He went on: *"I have tried this Jesus thing and I frankly do not believe it. I do not want to raise MY children as Christians anymore, so the children and I will be moving out as soon as possible."* There had been a sullen, brooding spirit hovering over him during the previous weeks but this conversation came as a total shock! He had always been so captivated by me. He had adored me! What happened? His old ways of manipulation and control were no longer effective when it came to my spiritual convictions. Was the threat of divorce a bullying tactic designed to make me deny Christ? Perhaps.

His mother had alienated herself from him by dogmatically forcing him to attend religious schools and the local Catholic University. When he refused to attend that university their relationship reached an impasse during his college years until I came along to help mend it. He had always been very sensitive about being nagged which stemmed from that relationship with his mother. This hadn't posed a problem for me. I wasn't a nag. But those old templates in his mind reacted to my Christian convictions. Strangely, it was while we were visiting his mother on that vacation that those ugly old templates resurfaced as familial spirits, making me the epitome of his childhood issues. In his mind, I had become his nagging mother trying to force religion down his unwilling throat!

DEMONIC SPIRITS   The ensuing days, weeks, and months were unbelievable! I became the enemy in my own home. Looking back now after so many years I am still astounded at how quickly the entire family turned against me. Even the neighborhood children who had always congregated at our house began to mock me. Demonic soul-power took over and Satan's evil wiles worked overtime demolishing the wholesome atmosphere in our home. Rebellion reigned. I didn't have the tools to know what to do, nor had I yet been schooled in spiritual warfare. I kept praying that things would get better, but they didn't.

Years later I learned about *Parental Alienation Syndrome*, sometimes referred to as *Malicious Parent Syndrome*, a good parent/bad parent condition in which the child often supports the bad parent throughout life. This is fostered by the bad parent constantly badmouthing the good parent, who is usually non-confrontational and does not adequately defend himself or herself. He may lie to the child about the other parent, may deny visitations, or fail to make required child support payments. Often the bad parent has a personality disorder that keeps him or her from responding rationally. The alienating parent may be punishing the other parent for *'wrong-doing'*. This could have been the case in our little family.

Sadly, the children become the victims of their divorcing parent's emotionally charged poor decisions and behavior. Although some of those *Parental Alienation Syndrome* symptoms were exhibited by my children's father I realize in retrospect that I could have handled some things more wisely, too. I deeply regret this. Perhaps my zeal for Jesus should have been tempered by more Godly wisdom, but given my upbringing, my lack of experience and guidance I did the best I could. The deck was stacked against me.

I tried to live by my principles especially by not speaking negatively against my husband to my parents or the children out of respect that he had been my husband and my children's father. This backfired when I later learned that Aria and Tim were reporting material to their father for his 'black book' which contained my *'misdoings'*. To this day I cannot imagine what tales that book contained. Nevertheless, I firmly believed I needed to set an example of not degrading or criticizing him. I knew that if I clutched the children to me as their father was pulling them to himself the pressure would be too much for them and they might snap just as if a rubber band was being pulled on both ends.

Sometimes true love requires the greater strength, just as is revealed in that poignant story of two mothers in 1 Kings 3:16-28. The two women came to Solomon after one of their babies died, both of them claiming that the remaining son was theirs. Solomon, in his undeniable wisdom, called for his sword, intent on resolving the dilemma. As he raised the sword to divide the baby in two, giving half to each mother, the true mother relented! Her love for her son insisted that the child's life be spared even if it would cost her the deep loss of raising him! Love revealed the truth.

We had purchased acreage up the coast of Maine and my husband had been telling the children for months that I no longer wanted to be part of the family; that I didn't want to be involved in the big adventure of building a new house together in the country. *"Mom doesn't want to be part of the family anymore. She just wants God,"* he would cruelly say. *"She loves God more than she loves you!"* I wasn't able to break through the painful lies that were being told against me or convince the children that still I adored them.

Then, on that horrendous, nightmare-ish day everything dear to me on earth rolled down the driveway in that shabby old station wagon! My dreams were shattered! I was in anguish, torn apart, heartbroken! How could I bear being separated from the children? Worst yet was that they were going off to the very environment I most dreaded for them; one in which God and the Bible were denounced and mocked! The secure home life, manners, and values they had been taught no longer would be encouraged. They were being taught to *think for themselves*; to challenge the principles they had been taught. Their strong foundation would be shattered. And Mom was foolish, moronic, and misguided by her Wizard-of-Oz God.

CHAPTER 3

NOW WHAT?

stood there in the driveway a long time looking off into the distance as scalding hot tears streamed down my face. I was numb. My family disappeared as if they were embarking on a typical outing; off for an afternoon's adventure almost as casually as if they would be home for supper. Only I wasn't included. And it wasn't about an adventure or the new house. Nor was it anymore about my foolishness, my not wanting to be 'part of the family' or not loving the kids as they had been told. No indeed! It was all about the kingdoms of light and darkness. At that moment I was too devastated to realize it; time would prove that I would win! I would win in so many ways and through it all, God would be glorified!

MEMORIES   Eventually I stumbled back into the house. I rambled from room to room, not knowing quite what to do with myself while dozens of memories flashed across my mind as though I were thumbing through pictures of an old photo album. I trudged up the stairs of our drafty, post-Victorian house to the children's rooms. Aria's room was first at the top of the stairs. Her bookshelf stood there proudly boasting her favorite books which had been carefully gathered from a myriad of thrift stores and garage sales. My darling girl was such a bookworm, always leaving a trail of books behind. I could almost see her cozily cuddled up in her empty big, old iron and brass bed decked out in its handmade puffy coverlet I had lovingly sewn for her. How I cherished the nightly devotion times we had shared in the peacefulness of her room. I could only hope that she would stay true to the commitment she had made to the Lord one night after reading the scripture, *"To all that did receive Him, to those who believed in His name, He gave the right to become the children of God"* (John 1:12).

That had been her very own revelation! Aria...my first born. The one doctors had told me I would never bear. Those words had provoked me to make promises to the Lord. *"Oh Lord, My wonderful Savior! I will not accept that prognosis! I will believe your good report and You will hear my prayers! I promise I will raise every child that You give me to know you. I promise!"*

Aria's generous, kind nature and keen intelligence were precursors to the brilliant physician she would one day become. She was my pride and joy. But now she felt the necessity to take care of Dad and to be the *'lady of his house'.* It would be many years before the hardness of her heart toward me would soften even a little bit. The sting of losing her was almost more than I could bear! I buried my face in her inviting bed pillows for a long time, overcome with sobs of despair!! A bottomless hollow pit was being excavated in the depths of my aching heart.

Eventually, I plodded down the hall to the boys' room. I remembered them engaging in one of their frequent brotherly pillow fights. Looking out their bedroom window to the garage below I was reminded of an evening not long before when the family car exploded in a blaze of fire due to an electrical problem. Only five minutes earlier the boys had been asleep in the back of the car exactly where the fire had broken out! What a testimony of God's faithfulness it was to me that He had assigned angles to watch over them to protect them from danger! That memory was comforting me now as I considered the life my boys were now facing! Surely my God would assign angels in this situation, too, to keep a watchful eye over them!

So many nights in that very bedroom I would succumb to the boys' demands that we play our game of *'count the bones'*! I would count one more spinal bone than the night before insisting that they had grown yet another bone and how they would giggle and ask for more!

I remembered one night in that very room when Tim was undressing to get ready for bed. I laughed so hard I thought my sides would burst when the nickels and dimes fell out of his shoes jingling onto the bedroom floor. I had warned him the night before that: *"Money burns a hole in your pocket"*!

That entrepreneurial spirit was a God-given gift, however. He had a business sense which would later manifest in a very creative manner, as owner/developer of a successful sailing school in Thailand. Tim was quick, agile, and usually ten steps ahead of most of us. What a gift he was, with a wrap-around-smile that would cheer up the most hardened cynic and a generous heart as big as the moon! He was indeed a free-spirit, always evading that proverbial butterfly net.

Even as he grew up to become a man Tim always was respectful around me to not use fowl or naughty words. Once I heard him say a naughty word and promptly took him to the bathroom to wash out his mouth with soap. I never recovered from the guilt of that experience. When a parent tells his child that *"It was harder on me than on you"*, it surely was in that case!

When he was only four years old he learned a naughty word which he decided to try out for himself by writing that word under the seat cushion on our living room sofa-bed. He spelled it correctly, too, but then it was only a four-letter-word! I discovered it as I was preparing the bed for a visit from my mother. That was when Tim got his first sewing lesson by stitching a big patch over the naughty word so Granny would not be horrified when she came for her visit the next week.

My mother's visit did have a strange twist, however, for which Tim was responsible. When she went to bed she slipped her new contact lenses into a glass of water which she had placed on a nearby shelf. In the morning Tim couldn't wait to see Granny, who lay there still fast asleep on the sofa-bed. Discovering the water sitting on the shelf near her bed he couldn't resist drinking the entire glassful, contact lens and all! Poor granny! She groped and stumbled the entire time she was with us because she didn't see well without her contacts! And little Tim was ashamed. I don't think she ever spent the night with us again!

That flood of sweet memories mixed with shock and disbelief that my children were gone produced emotions far too poignant to adequately describe. After sitting in the boy's room awhile I slowly wandered across the upstairs hall to the children's playroom still cluttered with toys. A wooden playhouse set up in the playroom had provided countless hours of fun. The children would turn it into a make-believe fort or a mysterious faraway castle with the simple addition of a blanket or a few blocks. I could just picture David engrossed in play. He got his share of my attention as the baby of the family. By the age of five, he had already demonstrated the sensitivity of the talented artist and musician he would one day become. He was so lovable, sensitive, and smart. I'm certain he had a photographic memory.

I hadn't realized how big and creaky the old house could be. Goosebumps sprouted all over me as noises I'd never before heard came out of nowhere ...creaky noises, shutters-banging noises, and wind-blowing-outside noises. As the first night settled in I felt soooo small and that old house suddenly became strangely bigger than ever ...and empty! Bearing my soul before the Lord, my tearful prayer that night went something like this:

"Lord, prove your faithfulness to me. I am going to need your strength now more than ever to survive! I am so scared and my faith is so weak! All my dreams are shattered! I don't know what to do! Put angels around my children; protect their emotions and keep them from every kind of harm!"

"My dear Jesus, you know this is so hard for me to surrender my children to what might be the worst atmosphere I could ever imagine for them. Give me the grace to trust that You will work even this to the good as Your Word promises!"

ARIA AND TIM – WE WERE SEPARATED FOR MANY YEARS

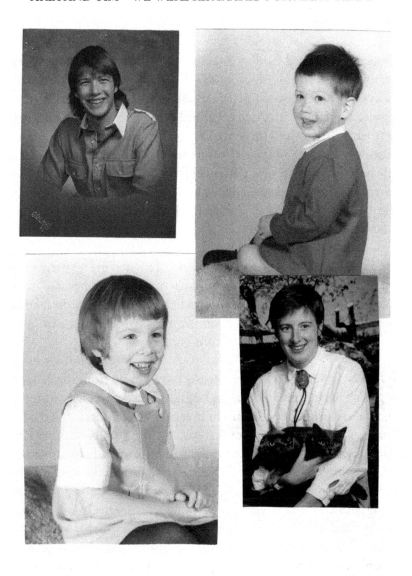

NEW FRIENDS   Of course, the Lord had been making plans for me. How could I have known the plans He all ready had for me; *"Plans for a hope and a future?"* (Jer. 29:11). How was I to know that by turning my world inside out my fearful self would become strong as I learned to trust Him? How could I have imagined that it was

25

possible to not only survive but even thrive beyond this devastating twist in my life?

I desperately needed God to intervene in some way to encourage me. Meeting the young family from my church in the supermarket a few weeks earlier was just the providential input I needed ...they would become my family in the days ahead. Our hearts were being knit together as we began to carpool to attend church services an hour's distance away. Lionel and Fonda, former hippies, were intent on building a life together in their new Christian faith. I fell in love with the pure-hearted passion of this beautiful couple and their adorable baby girl, Jolie. We became instant God-friends; the kind of friendship only God could have put together!

One afternoon shortly after my family left I invited my new friends to have supper with me. As fate would have it, the baby became inconsolably irritable and fussy. Fonda decided it would be best to take her home leaving Lionel behind to finish moving some items from my cellar to my garage for my upcoming garage sale.

LIONEL   As he was carrying the last item up from the cellar to my garage his knees buckled and he gracefully floated to the ground, as gentle as a feather floating in the breeze! His head landed in the bed of pansies I had planted earlier that spring. Strangely, I had always had a special sensitivity to that particular bed of pansies. Now those blossoms became a pansy-choir whose pretty smiling faces were looking heavenward singing praises to Jesus! How ironic that now Lionel was resting his head in that very bed of praise! Instinctively and immediately I sensed he was in the Lord's presence.

The ambulance rushed Lionel to the hospital while I raced to retrieve Fonda and Jolie to await the diagnosis. All too soon the doctor's report confirmed that indeed Lionel had died instantly of cardiac arrest at only 38 years of age!

What a fine line exists between our life on earth and our eternal destiny. Heaven is only a breath away! Oh! If we only would think of that more often as we walk out our days on earth. We would surely do some things differently! I remembered an old saying from my youth,

"Only one life, T'will soon be past.
Only what's done For Christ will last"!

FONDA   Fonda and Jolie returned to my home for the night. Exhausted, we begrudgingly traipsed up the open stairway in my home to finally retire for the night. As grief welled up like an immense balloon within us, the strangest event surprisingly turned the mood upside down. A bat from the pond across the street had found his way inside an open window and was expertly dive-bombing figure eight circles in the open stairway while we ascended to the second-story bedrooms. As the bat made nose-dives around us, Fonda, clutching Jolie in her arms, and I nearly trampled each other as we made a mad dash for the bathroom, slamming the door shut behind us. It was the first room in the upstairs hallway. Pausing to catch our breath we armed ourselves with bath towels to equip ourselves to continue our frantic trek down the hall to the bedroom, furiously flapping the towels above our heads to ward off the bat. Once in the bedroom with the door secure, we collapsed into fits of laughter. We laughed and laughed until our sides ached. Laughter came as a relief and released the built-up tension from the unexpected horror we had just experienced.

After such an explosion of laughter, the heart-wrenching emotional turmoil of the evening was somehow just not quite as severe. After tucking baby Jolie safely in a makeshift dresser drawer crib I prayed for Fonda to be spared the predictable grief she so dreaded. Fonda looked up, her eyes bright, *"Marjorie, something has lifted! There has been a shift!"* she announced that surprisingly the grief had been lifted. By the grace of God, miraculously it never again returned.

We had learned a new meaning of the word, *'temperance'.* In His grace, God sometimes brings relief by tempering a difficult situation through unusual circumstances, just as laughter had become the anecdote for the trauma we had just experienced. Despite the difficulties we both faced, Fonda and I frequently found ourselves experiencing something hilariously funny. We laughed like schoolgirls again and again.

This began a new chapter in both of our lives. Fonda never returned to live in loneliness in her apartment and I now had not only a roommate but an instant best friend who would become more than a sister to me. I suffered from frequent migraine headaches and issues causing me severe pain weeks out of every month. Fonda, in her kindness, would often bring a pot of tea by my bedside and pray for me. Our difficult circumstances carved out a capacity for such a deep friendship! No one would ever be a replacement for my family, but she would be God's provision in my life supplying friendship, support, and unconditional love during my chapter of adjustment. Nine years her senior, in some ways I became the mother substitute for her mother she lost at age six. And my example would serve her well years later when she had her own large combined family to mother.

BROKEN VESSEL   As days turned into weeks and then into months I was forbidden to see the children. My husband did not have a phone so I couldn't call. For months I had no contact with them. I was crazy-lonesome for my children. Life without my kids...who was I? I was a mother, but I had lost my children! It was a desperate time for me! Their father used his bully-ish ways to control me by not providing financial support. That first winter we survived on a diet of vegetables I had frozen from my garden, applesauce made from fallen apples I confiscated from a local schoolyard, and homemade whole wheat bread. Fonda paid a little rent and somehow we managed to survive! We drank a lot of tea!

God surely used this season in my life to squeeze me. I was aching for my children. The pain drew me closer to my Jesus. Like the woman in the bible whose broken alabaster box released its fragrant oil, my brokenness also released the sweetness of the Holy Spirit. I became more sensitive to other's losses and grievances. I was easily moved to tears. I often sensed the tender comfort of the Holy Spirit. A broken vessel is One that God can use. I wanted to linger in the Presence of Jesus; sit at His feet, let Him wipe away my tears.

THANKSGIVING When Thanksgiving rolled around rather than sit around and feel sorry for myself, I invited a dozen bible school students to my home to celebrate our blessings together! It was a *'by faith'* splurge as I spent nearly my entire grocery budget (which came from Fonda's scanty rent money) for the month on those groceries. What a celebration it was! My table wore it's finest damask linens and polished sterling silver. The recipes were carefully selected from those I had collected over the years. All the place settings were graced with a handwritten place card bearing a specific bible verse the Lord had given me for each one. As the guests found their seats there were squeals of delight all around the table. *"How did you know this was my favorite verse?"*, or *"This is my life-verse!"* or *"This verse is an answer to the prayer for wisdom I have been asking the Lord!"* Every single guest received a blessing from the Lord on his/her place card! Although I wasn't expecting the guests to bring anything, they brought so much food that there was ample provision for the entire month! He blessed us with such bounty!

My husband had installed a monstrous old wood stove in the middle of the house before he left, a hideous old contraption which I never seemed to be able to master. With no oil in the furnace, I did my best to stoke the old beast and keep the fires burning. But heating all the nooks and crannies of a big old Victorian house with a wood stove was not very effective through that long Maine winter. My normally small frame evolved into a rotund barrel as I usually wore most of my clothes all at once; layers, layers, and more layers of warm clothes! But as winter progressed I became acclimated to the cold and didn't fight the old wood stove so much. Eventually, the long winter passed.

Then...a wonderful thing happened.

DAVID'S VISIT To this very day I do not know what motivated my husband to allow six-year-old David to come for a visit that warm Spring weekend. But I was crazy-giddy-ecstatic about his upcoming visit and did all I could to make it a memorable occasion! A celebration! What a reunion we had!

During his visit, I needed to run a quick errand to the auto supply store. Who could have imagined the twist the story would take as a result. The motor-cycle helmet display caught David's eye, stopping him in his tracks! He suddenly became obsessed with the idea of owning and wearing one of those fine, shiny helmets! He begged and cajoled that I would buy one for him!

Had it been in my power, I surely would have given him the moon! Sadly, however, my limited funds curbed any frivolous spending! He insisted. But it was an impossible request for me to fulfill, as much as I wanted to spoil him! He was so disappointed. It broke my heart that I couldn't give him that which he wanted so badly!

Returning him to his dad's at the weekend's close, I had trouble finding the right words to comfort him. *"My David, you know Mommy wanted to get that beautiful helmet for you."* I stammered. How could I console my hurting child? *"But your heavenly Father in heaven owns the cattle on a thousand hills (Ps. 50:10), and there is nothing too hard for Him! I shall surely be talking to Him about this all week!"*

My prayers were red-hot that week as I petitioned my Lord! I passionately pleaded with steady persistence. Remembering the scripture, *"You have not because you ask not"* (James 4:2), indeed I was asking! This was surely the test of my faith! If ever there were passionate, heartfelt requests made to the throne of God, it would be those prayers of this broken-hearted mother interceding for her child.

My prayer started something like this:

"My dear Father, If you never answer another prayer of mine, this is the ONE that matters more than anything!" I retreated to my prayer closet that week petitioning the loving Father for a special motorcycle helmet for a very dear and unique boy, my David! This prayer was not a petition for some frivolous present to spoil my child. No! It was about a desperate young mother bombarding the Kingdom of God to display the love and generosity of God the Father to a confused little boy. My rocket-prayers bombarded the throne room that week! They were:

Relentless,
      Persistent,
           Passionate,
                Full-of-faith
                    AND DESPERATE!

And I told NO ONE about my fervent petitions!! The answer came in quite an unpredictable way.

Early in the week two brothers, former neighbors, came to my door bearing a good-sized package. They had been enjoying one of their favorite pastimes of *'dump picking'* when they stumbled upon a new, unopened, plastic-wrapped, child-sized (you guessed it!) motorcycle helmet! The elder brother became the spokesman: *"Marjorie, we found this great child's motorcycle helmet while we were dump-picking. We immediately thought of your little boy, but didn't know if you would accept something we found at the dump."* With great enthusiasm, he was just getting started. *"Since it was unopened and still in its protective cover we hoped you would accept it. You know your son and I are both named 'David', so I have a particular affection for him. Do you think he would like this? You wouldn't be offended, would you?"*

Offended? I nearly yanked the package from their loose grip! With trembling hands, I pulled off the sealed wrapper as I related to them that they were an answer to my most heartfelt, fervent prayer! I told them I was expecting a motorcycle helmet but didn't know how it would come. This was quite a testimony of God's faithfulness to the brothers, who were not yet believers.

As I waited for David's visit it seemed as though that Friday would never come! His visit would be like a Christmas morning! I was giddy-impatient! No little boy ever had a more wonderful surprise waiting for him... directly from God the Heavenly Father! Eventually, that awaited Friday came! David's dear little-boy hands anxiously dove into the waiting package, revealing the coveted prize! This was no ordinary motorcycle helmet. No indeed! Rather, it was a child-sized helmet with a unique built-in walkie-talkie! It was tailor-made just for him!

It would have been a delight for any six-year-old, but to David, it was the absolute ultimate! He wore the helmet constantly, right along with his accompanying ear-to-ear smile. This brought such joy to my heart!

The memory of his bedtime ritual that night will forever be vivid in my mind. The words he whispered to me just before he drifted off to sleep, with his cherished helmet tucked in next to him, still rings clearly in my ears, *"Mommy, I love my new helmet! But how did you know I wanted a walkie-talkie? That was what I always wanted more than anything, even more than the helmet!"* he confided straight from his tender heart. *"BUT I NEVER, EVER TOLD ANYONE!"*

Even today, many years later it brings tears to my eyes when I consider the miracle I had just experienced because of the pity and concern of my loving Father. His compassion met the secret desires of a hurting little boy. That motorcycle helmet became a tool in David's life to bring him to the Lord. What may seem like a trivial coincidence in the life of my child was a kingdom issue straight from the Throne of God. I still vividly remember tenderly answering my darling child as I kissed him goodnight, *"God knew, my Little One, God knew."*

YOUNG DAVID

CHAPTER 4

TRANSITION

Whether it was the motorcycle helmet event or David directly telling his dad he wanted to live with Mommy, I may never know, but he returned home to live with me right after that. This surely spared me from experiencing the depths of broken-heartedness. He wasn't quite the same boy when he came home as when he had left, because unfortunately, he wore the effects of having been in an ungodly household for months. Some of those effects continued for years proving the powerful negative force of demonic activity and the influence of ungodly soul-ties.

SOUL POWER   As the father of lies, Satan would choose to attack through a dumb spirit since David was an unusually bright child. Ironically, even until he was in high school a dumb spirit would manifest itself upon David whenever his father posted a letter to him. Usually, I could tell when the letter was actually in the mail before it ever got to our house. Sometimes I wasn't perceptive enough to realize that this was the old enemy at work again. A day or two might have passed with an irritating undercurrent disrupting our household. After taking stock I would remember that a letter from David's father had recently arrived. I would conduct spiritual warfare by pleading the blood of Jesus over my child gaining victory over the nasty enemy once again!

Because Satan is very real and wants to get a foothold into our families in any way possible, he constantly is looking for an *'open door'* through which he might sneakily enter. Should the enemy invade, our Lord has equipped us with spiritual artillery with which to conduct warfare and clear the atmosphere.

Children are very susceptible to both good and evil spiritual activity, especially very sensitive and bright children. They may experience angelic visitations, have heavenly dreams, or hear a word from God, as well as be vulnerable to demonic activity. I have seen a child's high fever or his simply viewing undesirable television shows regularly, become an open door for demonic activity. A parent's fiercely strong anti-God antagonism may give a place for the unseen demonic realm to work through the child. Emotions, mind and will compose the soul of an individual. When an individual is born again, his soul begins to submit to his spirit. Without Godly submission, the soul can powerfully dominate. When an individual is at war with God his soulish side can exert great negative influence over others as in the case of voodooism. This *'soul-power'* continued to be a controlling force in my family for many years...that old *'principalities and powers'* principle (Eph. 6:12).

ANNE'S WORD FOR ME   Just a few days before the scheduled divorce hearing a dear, elderly friend, Anne, phoned me with a word she felt was from the Lord. I valued her words of wisdom and spiritual gifting. The youngest of twelve children, she left her home in Scotland as a young woman to become a missionary to China. After several years of passionately serving the Lord war broke out and she became a Chinese prisoner of war. That harrowing experience left her with a serious lifelong disease, disfiguring her once beautiful face. This kept her dependent upon the Lord for her daily strength. Later when Anne was hospitalized in Scotland the Lord spoke to Nedda, her highly trained specialized Scottish nurse, that her destiny was to care for Anne for the rest of her earthly life. So Anne and Nedda lived an unusual life of faith together trusting God for every provision, demonstrating the mighty power of God to others through a powerful ministry of prayer, counsel, and home Bible studies. The Lord's generous faithfulness to them was an inspiration to me in those days as I was learning to deepen my walk of faith. I would often become their chauffeur driving them to run their errands, always receiving much more than I had given to them!

That call from Anne just before the divorce hearing jolted me to the core! She spoke in her charming Scottish brogue, *"My dear, the Lord has put you on my heart these days."* There was a serious tone in her voice that conveyed an urgency to pay close heed to what she had to say. *"I have been in much prayer for the divorce hearing, Marjorie. Have you yielded to the Lord that His will be done?"*

Anne very gently suggested that I needed to lay my children on the altar before the Lord, to let Him direct the judge's heart in ruling for their custody. *"The heart of the king (judge) is in the hand of the Lord"* (Prov. 21:9 NKJV).

I had been so certain that God would award me full custody that I hadn't stopped to consider that the judge might rule to the contrary. Perhaps I didn't want to face that possibility. In brokenness, I lay my heart at His feet that night before the hearing. It surely was the most difficult heart-wrenching night of my life; that night when I yielded my children's future at the feet of Jesus. Oh! The agony of facing the pain of a possible life removed from my beloved children! It wasn't just about me losing them, but it broke my heart to consider that the atmosphere in which they might go would be refuting everything I had tried to instill in them all their young lives. In that prone position of brokenness I wrestled until at last I could honestly whisper, *"Lord, if this is the place where my children can best learn of You, or the place that will ultimately cause them to surrender fully to YOU...then..."* with tears flowing like a fountain ...*"I surrender"!* I was undone! Although it had been a struggle that wrung my heart inside out, at last I came to that place of full surrender. And strangely, in my brokenness, I was filled with the peace that passes understanding!

DIVORCE HEARING   The divorce hearing came and went. The judge awarded me custody of all three children. I was puzzled that their father only made an effort to get custody of the boys. If Aria would just bide her time eventually *'dear old dad'* would go back to court to fight for a custody change for her. Thankfully I was not aware that was their game plan just then. A couple of years later when she turned fourteen, the age at which a child in Maine could testify in court with which parent they choose to live, that plan became crystal clear.

Aria had returned home some months before the actual divorce hearing because quite frankly her father just didn't know how to deal with a budding twelve year-old young lady. She came back full of anger towards me. She was hurting and confused. But try as I may I was at a loss to know how to penetrate her bitterness and rebellion.

Following the hearing, I was elected to pick up Tim to bring him home. He was outraged, shouting obscenities to me that I was ruining his life by making him leave *his home with Dad*. Years later as an adult he continued carrying anger that made him leave the life he loved. Even though he returned to my home, his bitterness toward me and anger at the situation posed many problems. Aria, too, was fuming! Mom and her fanaticism! Our home pulsated with an atmosphere of animosity! I simply couldn't penetrate that hurt and bitterness with the deep love I had for my hurting children. The lies of Satan had so disrupted our family!

NEW HOUSE   By the time the divorce was finalized it became increasingly evident that leaving Portland might be a healthy new start for the children and me. I had begun running my errands at night because my ex-husband's lies about me had so tarnished my reputation that I was embarrassed to run into any of our former friends or neighbors. Our church had established a bible college in the Berkshire Mountains in Massachusetts. It seemed that relocating there with the children would provide a much needed fresh start.

I found a Post Victorian three-family house for sale which would allow me to make monthly mortgage payments with the rent I collected from the two small apartments. With a little time and elbow grease I knew I could transform the shabby, old beast into something quite comfortable and charming. Fonda and Jolie would be close at hand renting one of the downstairs apartments. Although the divorce settlement had provided funds for a meager down payment, what bank would give a mortgage to a single woman, new to town, unemployed with no work history or local references? Knowing the odds were stacked against me my realtor insisted that I get my parents to co-sign the loan.

With the children in Maine for the summer I reluctantly traveled to Seattle to summon my parent's assistance. My independent nature (or perhaps it was pride) had not previously permitted me to ask them for financial help. I had been fiercely independent. This request definitely went against my better judgment, but I felt desperate that this was my only alternative. Because my strong convictions did not allow me to speak negatively to them about my husband, they hadn't heard all the details of the failure of our marriage. They should have been supportive of me as their daughter regardless of those circumstances. They were not believers so I couldn't expect them to understand the spiritual nature of the battle I had been going through.

Upon my arrival to their home, my dad became quite ill and disappeared to his sickbed for nearly the duration of my visit. Finally he surfaced just before I was to return, flatly and angrily refusing to co-sign or provide any financial support. The Lord had protected me from his rebuke and anger for most of the visit, but his last minute demonstration of wrath left me feeling dejected and wounded!

I returned home emotionally drained, disappointed and suffering from a nasty ear infection with which I was riddled with pain and confined to my sick-bed for a week. The inevitable phone call I had to make to my realtor saying I had no co-signer left me feeling like I had failed in my mission! She didn't have much hope I would be awarded the loan without a co-signer! What was I to do? The odds were stacked against me even greater than before. Yet the Lord, in His infinite mercy began to penetrate my self-pity.

"Marjorie, my child, Oh ye of little faith. Is my arm too short to supply your every need? If you'd had faith to believe me for your provision, you would have been spared the heartache of that disappointing trip to your

parents. And my provision for you would bring Me glory, too. Trust me and see what I will do."

I realized I had limited the Lord. I had been trying to solve my dilemma my own way, or the way the realtor thought I should. I felt ashamed, yet challenged! I would trust Him to give me the faith to believe for our house loan to be approved. My circumstances had backed me into a corner. But God would not fail me. My sick-bed became my altar of prayer! I hung onto His promises with the tenacity of a pit-bull! My faith was getting stronger. Instead of speaking to God about my problem, I started speaking to those problems about my God! And I declared His Word:

"Trust in the Lord with all your heart and lean not unto your own under-standing, In all your ways submit to Him and He will make your paths straight" Prov. 3:5-6).

"Take delight in the Lord and He will give you the desires of your heart" (Ps. 37:4).

"My God will meet all your needs according to the riches of His glory in Christ Jesus Christ Jesus!" (Phil. 4:19).

"Ah Lord God, You have made the heavens and earth by Your great power and outstretched arm; <u>nothing is too hard for You</u>" (Jer. 32:17).

He miraculously answered my prayers! He not only supplied the grace to wait, but down-loaded a big dose of His faith, too. The grace and faith preceded the miracle, of course; essential to equip me for days ahead when I would need to know how to access those tools again. I was learning how to believe BIG! I was learning that faith is the cur-rency of heaven!

The victory-call from the realtor came none too soon! She was com-pletely dismayed that the bank had approved me, admitting that she had just witnessed a miracle! Once again, He had answered my prayers. It seemed that He enjoyed putting me in impossible situations just so

He could demonstrate His power. I was just a vessel through which He could write His story! I would say to Him, *"Lord, let me make you famous!"*

With the children coming back in only four weeks we had a house to beautify! Together Fonda and I refinished floors, set tile, replaced a ceiling and painted, painted and painted. We made lists and kept to our schedule. Amidst our giggles we hung wallpaper precariously balanced over the steep stairwell. Using my steam iron we ingeniously lifted the old linoleum off the kitchen floor to expose beautiful maple underneath. We worked day and night, praising the Lord all the while! Faithfully, the Lord energized us to finish our work just in time to surprise the children with a freshly re-decorated home ready to start a new chapter.

CUTTING "FAITH TEETH"   Those days were school days for me, days in which I cut my *faith teeth*. The Lord faithfully provided many opportunities for me to do so. I trusted God with all that was in me for financial provision and for blessings for my little family. I had nothing to hang onto but my faith and how tenaciously and passionately I hung on! I discovered that faith is not merely belief. Belief is passive. Faith is active. So I had to learn to put action to my belief to elevate it to become faith.

The children returned from their vacation in Maine and we began to adjust to our new life together in Massachusetts. Because I had been so diligent to get the house ready for the kid's homecoming. Aria's first comments after making a detailed inspection of our decorating efforts were very hurtful, *"I would be ashamed to bring my friends home to a house that still needs paint on the outside."*

The sting of those and other hurtful words from my family penetrated so deeply. I am reminded that our words are mighty and powerful, having tremendous influence over our lives and the lives of others. I would struggle in that battle of hurtful words for a very long time. It was incongruous that she would make such a statement having just come from her Dad's home-under-construction that didn't even have a flush toilet or shower. But, of course, that had been an adventure. In Aria's mind I was the culprit who had disrupted our family. Tim, also, had a growing rebellion toward me believing that if he were nasty enough I would permit him to go back to Maine to live in the woods with his dad. I had become the enemy. How would I be able to retrieve them from this snare of rebellion and distrust? I held onto my faith with a fierce determination.

Those days were school days for me, days in which I cut my *faith teeth.* The Lord faithfully provided many opportunities for me to do so. I trusted God with all that was in me for financial provision and for blessings for my little family. I had nothing to hang onto but my faith and how tenaciously and passionately I hung on! I discovered that faith is not merely belief. Belief is passive. Faith is active. So I had to learn to put action to my belief to elevate it to become faith.

Surely, the new life I was determined to carve out for the children and me would renew their sense of security and restore our relationship. Time would heal our wounds. I was certain that the Lord would bring victory! This new beginning became another opportunity for me to deepen my faith roots and watch the Lord supply our needs.

With the decorating behind us and the children settled into their respective schools, it was now time for me to begin my job search, this being the last piece of the puzzle to complete our new life in Massachusetts. Although I'd had good secretarial skills at one time, I hadn't worked outside the home since the children had come along. Mustering up my confidence and girded with prayer, I put my trust in God and His promises and began my job search with confidence. At that time the economy where we had moved was dominated by one industry. Ironically this company had just laid off a high percentage of their employees as a result of a recession! My job search became a nightmare of rejection and disappointment that I hadn't counted on! Although the income from my two little rental units covered our mortgage, there were other expenses. The coffers were emptying all too quickly. My faith and confidence were being challenged.

CATERING BUSINESS   As the holidays approached the children were quick to remind me that there would not be money for Christmas gifts if I didn't get work soon. As one door after another shut I started to think creatively about ways to provide an income. As I took stock of my talents and abilities a light bulb flickered. Along came a brilliant idea...a gourmet catering business hosting small intimate dinner parties! Of course! I couldn't wait to brainstorm with Fonda. What we may have lacked in experience we could surely make up for in determination and faith. With God guiding us we turned our idea into a reality.

I would prepare the meals with all the trimmings and Fonda would be in charge of making hot hors d'oevres. Fonda was quick to remind me, *"Of course, you know that I have never made an hors d'oevre, Marjorie",* she insisted, to which I responded, *"But you can read the cookbook instructions!"* We worked out all the details. We made our way to the local library to collect just-right recipes, assembled a group of appetizing menus written in Fonda's fine calligraphy, sewed long matching hostess aprons and readied ourselves for our *marketing campaign".* Hilariously, our *marketing campaign,* limited because of our lack of funds, meant *hitting the streets*! So we *hit the streets* determined to land a client.

With menus in hand we pushed Baby Jolie ahead of us in her rickety stroller through a fresh blanket of snow! Our enthusiasm began to wane as we witnessed one rejection after another. At last, a hopeful candidate somewhat reluctantly invited us inside her beautiful home, rescuing us from the bitter frosty winter air. She seemed to be relieved to hear of the services we offered! *"A holiday buffet would be the perfect solution to our many social obligations! There would be about a hundred doctors and their spouses on my guest list!"* My head was spinning! Although I had never personally prepared a meal for more than a mere dozen guests my desperation compelled me to heartily accept without hesitation! I was beginning to see that when God opens a door it may take courage to walk through it.

I immediately trotted to the local Jewish caterer showing him the same menu I had presented to my client asking for a quote as if this were to be my party. I could undercut his price and still make a profit. I would prepare my bid and acquire a client! Imagine my delight to later discover all my grocery receipts tallied within fifty cents of my estimated costs. The Lord was honing my business sense even then.

Our efforts were a smashing success! One rotund James Beardian-type physician's spouse spent the evening hovering over the buffet table gorging himself with immense pleasure. The stuffed mushrooms so intrigued him that he actually tracked me down in the kitchen determined to pry the recipe from me. Through stifled giggles we refused to share the recipe saying it was a business secret. After he returned to the buffet table Fonda and I broke out in hilarious laughter knowing that the secret, unexpected ingredient which had piqued his curiosity was nothing more than Gerber's strained beef baby food! I simply couldn't admit that!

A group of neighbor ladies humbly showed up in the kitchen admitting in unison that they had been putting doubt in the hostess's mind about whether we had reliable references or would even show up for the event. There had been cynical refusals at each of their doors a few weeks earlier. After making solemn apologies a couple of these busy bodies actually contracted for us to cater their own upcoming events! And most rewarding of all, our hostess and her husband demonstrated their gratitude by graciously extending an invitation for us to enjoy their summer island home any week of that summer, complete with the use of the family SUV. Wow! Walking by faith is the way to go!

BLOCK ISLAND GET-AWAY   So the week of July 4th Fonda, Jolie, David and I boarded a small private plane to fly to Block Island off the shore of Rhode Island at the generosity of our dear hosts. A real vacation was a rare pleasure for us, so we with left with high spirits and excited anticipation. We were given instructions to be on the lookout for the lost family pet who by some slim chance might show up. Just before the family had left the island on their last visit thirty days earlier their beloved Cockapoo was nowhere to be found. With heavy hearts and their flight's departure to the mainland imminent they sadly gave up their exhaustive search.

After unpacking our bags and inspecting our luxurious new digs we made our way to the daylight basement garage to explore the island in the waiting SUV. *"Fonda, quickly come to see what I just discovered!"* I shrieked as I opened the car door! Imagine our shock and surprise to discover the missing little canine, panting with short breaths and curled up the front seat barely alive! Because the garage was under the house the SUV had been spared the hot summer sun. The little fellow had eaten the upholstery off the doors in an effort to try to escape and probably had kept alive by licking the condensation off the windows. He wouldn't have survived much longer, but after plenty of water and a few good meals he rallied, becoming our devoted and inseparable companion during our stay. As dog lovers ourselves his constant friendship was a delight to us, but paled in comparison to the joy his return home brought his owners!

Taking a step of faith by moving out of my comfort zone and knocking on a few doors resulted in being able to pay my outstanding bills and make a wonderful Christmas for my kids. The Lord empowered me to do something for which I had no experience or skill whatsoever! And the business skills and ingenuity He had begun to hone in me would serve me well in the months and years to come.

CHAPTER 5

DIVINE OPPORTUNITY

My anxiety was mounting. I discovered that using my home kitchen as the base for my budding catering business was not in compliance with city codes. I didn't have the necessary start-up funds to rent a kitchen or advertise. So my catering business with only three or four events under its belt was short-lived.

DESPERATION   One evening just before Christmas I found myself pouring out my heart to Fonda over a cup of tea in her tiny kitchen. *"Fonda, I need a breakthrough! There just don't seem to be any answers about how I am going to support myself and my little family. This recession makes getting a job impossible!"* I continued my pity party, *"The kids are really getting under my skin, too! They keep badgering me that if I don't get a job soon they won't have any Christmas presents! They are so worried!"* I was beginning to wonder if moving to Massachusetts had been a mistake! Of course, the devil always looks for an opportunity to cause fear and anxiety. By opening the door to doubt and insecurity I had unknowingly invited a whole lot of other vermin to torment me. Where had my faith gone?

In her usual gracious style, Fonda knew just what to do! That was when she put the water on to boil to prepare a hot pot of tea for us! It is amazing how comforting a hot cup of tea can be! As we sipped our tea we spoke words of faith to encourage ourselves in the Lord. Sometimes it is a good idea to simply encourage oneself in the Lord, to recall His promises and faithfulness from past victories. This sets the stage for more effective, powerful prayer by building faith! With hearts quiet and our faith encouraged we promptly bombarded the throne of heaven with persistent petitions for provision. How we poured out our hearts! The Lord had been faithful in so many, many ways as I had put my trust in Him. He would surely not fail me now! It is so comforting to truly know that He hears and answers every prayer; that we can go boldly to the throne of grace with our concerns and petitions!

Fonda insisted that to cheer us up she would break tradition by opening one of her few Christmas gifts early. As the ribbon and wrapping fell to the floor a trio of beautifully packaged cosmetics emerged. Although the gift was for Fonda, just the sight of this beautiful gift was promising encouragement! Following my hunch and leaving no stone unturned I copied the address from the labels. That night before bed I penned a brief note to the manufacturer asking how to distribute these lovely products. God knew that I had always had a weakness for skin-care products! Who could have predicted the ensuing chapter that would follow as a result of hastily jotting that *'insignificant'* little note before bed?

The weeks between Christmas and Valentine's Day continued to test my faith. My job search became exhaustingly futile as we all too quickly devoured the remaining fumes in my bank account. I claimed His promises, proclaimed victory, and waited upon the Lord, who had promised in His Word to renew my strength. And my strength was surely in need of renewal!

With Aria's fourteenth birthday approaching the end of January, the age a child could testify in court which parent with whom they chose to live, I was coming to grips with the fact that she would be moving back to the Maine woods with her dad. Heartbroken, I reluctantly allowed her to go back because I didn't want her to go through life with the guilt of falsely testifying in court against her mother. Before Aria was born doctors had told me I would never be able to bear children. That news had devastated me! Motherhood was my destiny! I had bargained and pleaded with God that if only He would let me have children I would raise them to serve Him.

I knew in my heart after Aria left for Maine that it would only be a matter of time before Timmy would be on her heels following right along behind her, too. His growing inward anger percolated into a boiling rebellion that he demonstrated on every occasion. Was this my sweet Tim, my boy that had been so full of love and kindness? I feared that if he continued in such rebellion it would become so deeply engraved that it would shape a life-long mindset causing him great harm throughout his life! I overheard his father coach him that if he were rebellious enough I wouldn't be able to handle him and would eventually give in to his demands to move back to Maine. Tim had eagerly complied.

Sadly, that winter at the young age of twelve Timmy returned to Maine. For years whenever I would see a young boy about his current age, momentarily I would instead visualize my dear *'Timmus'*. Tears would flood my eyes and my heart would ache all over again. Many a night I awoke to find my pillow damp from tears shed over my beloved children. I would hold them up to the Lord and He would comfort me assuring me that He loved them more than I could. Trusting the Lord in this area would be a lifelong struggle.

I had done my best to teach my kids about Jesus and to honor God. I adored them and had built a wholesome family life as a rich foundation for them. What had gone awry? He was quick to remind me that the story was not yet over, that He had a redemptive plan. Part of that plan was to teach me to trust Him.

I thought of Hannah's desperate prayers to have a child, promising to commit him to the Lord and ultimately surrendering her beloved son, Samuel, to the Lord. And with a heavy heart, I remembered the words my Lord had whispered to me years before,

"Have you counted the cost?

46

DOUBLE LOSS

COMFORT   I found strength and comfort in the words David the shepherd boy sang when life's difficulties were too much for him to bear alone: *"When my heart is overwhelmed lead me to the Rock that is higher than I"* (Ps. 61:2 NKJV). My problems weren't immediately fixed, but my heart found a place to go; to rest and be renewed when the overwhelming thoughts came.

DIVINE MEETING   Through the Lord's providential guidance I met a lady who became a stepping stone in God's unique destiny for me. She was a darling Roman Catholic nun who belonged to a liberal plain-clothes order which allowed a lot of flexibility and independence. Surprisingly she had recently become involved in selling Amway products. Isn't that crazy? Like so many others involved in multi-level marketing programs she exuded a contagious enthusiasm for the organization! Because of her encouragement and zeal, I followed her prompting, signed up, bought my starter kit, and began attending their rah-rah group meetings. Although I couldn't muster any enthusiasm to sell laundry soaps and cleaning products, I was indeed fascinated by the clever business structure which provided the opportunity to earn an override from the sales of those *'downline.'* This method was ingenious! I had never heard anything like it! I was uncertain if I could sell those boxes and bottles of cleaning products, but I had indeed caught the vision for building a multi-level structure business!

Alas, time proved that selling the Amway product line was NOT for me. Although the quality of the merchandise was first-class, I didn't have the enthusiasm to sell them. I had never been one to stock my cupboards with a lot of cleaning products, preferring the simplicity and effectiveness of tried and true good old vinegar, ammonia, and elbow grease. After many feeble attempts, I finally decided that this was just not my calling, packed up my sales kit, and continued my job search.

True to His Word the Lord continued to provide for us in unbelievable ways. An unexpected refund check showed up in my mailbox. One last catering job surfaced; this one for a nationally recognized writer in a nearby community. But, just when it seemed as if the well had run dry along came the life-changing infamous phone call from Jean King! It truly was a *kairos* moment!

ENTER JEAN KING   Jean lived on the other side of the state. My nearly forgotten letter-of-curiosity to the cosmetic company at Christmastime had been forwarded to Ms. King, a company manager. Since there were no representatives yet in the western part of the state, the company was especially happy to learn of my interest. Ms. King explained some of the details of the company, which was coincidentally structured as a multi-level organization, explaining my exposure to the business structure of the Amway Corporation. Ms. King wondered if I might be interested in having her come that Sunday to register as a *'skincare consultant'* and to hostess my first Skin Care class. Without hesitation, I enthusiastically agreed, *"Absolutely! And while you are at it why not bring a few extra start-up kits, just in case"*!

The following Sunday afternoon several friends from my church gathered in my living room while Jean gave a convincing skincare class demonstration. We all became immediate converts to the beautiful products and Jean eagerly signed up all five of my guests under my leadership becoming the newest skincare consultants in the company! As a play on Jean's name we called ourselves *'The King's Daughters'*, but the real inspiration for my branch's name was from the scripture: *"The king's daughters are all glorious within"* (Ps. 45:13 NKJV). Now began the challenge of marketing the product.

BATTLING INSECURITY   Enthusiasm for the appealing product line and packaging was easy for me. But the home party format was a very hard pill for me to swallow! The Lord had always been very patient with my mindsets, which sometimes needed to be dealt with to receive His best for me. I most definitely had an opinion about the home-party format! Inviting people to one's home expecting them to buy something didn't seem to fit my idea of being a gracious hostess. Besides, applying the skincare products to my guest's faces just plain seemed creepy and went against my admittedly snooty ideas. I began to doubt my ability to go through with this challenge. *"Lord, maybe I acted too hastily. You know I am just not cut out for this sort of thing.*

Please open the door for me to get a regular 'job' "I cajoled and squirmed, fumed, and fussed!

Speaking before a group of ladies and demonstrating the products terrified me so much that the wild butterflies in my stomach made me wonder if I could even do a class without getting sick! This was so far from my comfort zone! In fact, with increasing nausea mounting I surely would have canceled that first class had I not been so desperate to pay my outstanding bills! What had I gotten myself into? How could I stand and speak before all those ladies? I wasn't prepared for this! Had I made a mistake?

So, although my faith seemed distant, I faced the challenge ahead of me and just plain did it scared! But I did it! Fear can't stand faith and always tries to cancel it. Somehow, by the grace of God, I got through that scary first home party without throwing up! To my wonder, I came home with a surprisingly handsome booty! The Lord must have smiled at my squirming knowing full well that this was just the beginning of a very big blessing He had designed for me! One home party seemed to lead to another and before long my calendar was booked...and my fear was slowly evaporating!

Despite the impossibility of finding employment during a recession, despite my lack of work experience, and despite my stubborn opinions and fears, God once again honored my mustard-seed faith and accomplished the impossible! During those difficult years when so many obstacles stood in my path I found great comfort and strength from the verse, *"Ah Lord God, You have made the heavens and the earth by Your great power and outstretched arm. What can be too hard for You?"* (Jer. 32:17). When I was overwhelmed with life's challenges I would look at the awesome universe He had created and somehow it put my problems in perspective. I would wait for Him to perform the impossible once again.

MY PLEDGE   Throughout my marriage it had always troubled me that I hadn't been in a position to tithe since I did not have my own income and my husband was not a believer. After my divorce, I looked forward to the day when I would have an income from which to give to the Lord's work. It dawned on me that with careful planning the income generated from the sales of my skin-care classes could provide enough to meet our simple needs. Once I qualified to become a manager my *override* would then become a bonus. Now I had an opportunity to contribute generously to the Lord's work with my bonus check. *"Lord, thank you so much for making a way for me to help our start-up church in England. Right now I am pledging my monthly 'override' as an offering to help support that team!"*

This brainstorm so inspired me that I now was on a mission to build a powerful *'downline'* from which to collect that *'override'*. Since the cosmetic company didn't promote their multi-level structure very aggressively, having had the brief exposure to Amway definitely paid off! I now had a vision! With the Lord's help and hard work, I would bring it to pass! Little did I know just then what would be the result of that vision!

I recruited many of the women from my church and Bible college. Many of these women caught *the vision,* too, and were inspired to sell the products knowing that a portion of every sale would go to our Great Britain team. I enrolled one of my Portland friends and she caught the vision, too! Soon western Maine was on the company's map as her *'downline'* was competing with mine! I would keep my group motivated with regular meetings and bonuses, but the real motivator was our beloved team in England, passionately struggling to spread the gospel. Imagine my joy when in no time at all my growing *'downline'* produced an override that exceeded the earnings from my classes!

There is a scripture that says, *"Without a vision, the people perish!"* (Prov. 29:18 KJV). It stands to reason therefore that the opposite would be true as well. (*"With a vision, the people prosper!"*) That was true in my case. I became energized and motivated! So much so that I qualified as a manager, earning that valued override, in less time than any other previous employee in the history of the company! That's what the fire of the Holy Spirit can accomplish when He empowers an individual with the driving power of a Vision!

51

CHURCH LADIES BLOSSOM   Soon it became evident that the ladies in my church and Bible college using the product were reaping the benefits of good skincare. As their skin tone improved the ladies started to take more of an interest in their appearance resulting in better grooming and weight control! Although I hadn't intended to impact the church in this manner, the mushrooming positive effect that the introduction of the skin-care products had on our church ladies was incredible! Gradually, a rather dowdy group of ladies not only began to have increased self-esteem, but they also began to look a whole lot better! In addition, I emerged as a leader among women, which was a benefit I could never have imagined! And, an ordinary young woman with an extraordinary God began to blossom, too. The Lord works in mysterious ways His wonders to perform! How could I have known that He was planting seeds within me to become a women's ministry leader and speaker in years to come.

RAH-RAH MEETING   Shortly after Tim left for the Maine woods David's return home from school one afternoon found me perched atop a step ladder hanging wallpaper in our back hallway. Prophetically, I announced to him, *"Get ready; we are about to embark on a great adventure!"* I told him that God had an exciting plan for us, although I had no clue what it would be. That statement was surprising and unpremeditated, so when the adventure materialized my impulsive comment began to make sense!

As was the case with many other multi-level marketing organizations it was customary for my company to host periodic 'rah-rah' meetings in a fine hotel setting. These occasions would be complete with a motivational speaker to encourage the skincare consultants and their managers, in addition to emphasizing and strengthening the company's identity. That fall a motivational meeting was scheduled in Albany, NY to which I had been invited. I would be recognized for my accomplishments in the organization. Fonda and I decided to make a special event out of it, donned our finest apparel, and made the road trip to Albany. Little did we realize how that very event would be yet another "fork in the road", a defining, *kairos* moment!

BIRTHING THE VISION   At the last minute the scheduled guest speaker had an emergency, so the company's general manager from California addressed the guests in his stead. His address was probably pretty predictable, but when he began to announce that the company was breaking new ground in several foreign countries, my ears promptly perked up! *"...Holland, Brazil, Canada, and <u>England</u>"* he crowed. When he called out *'England'*, my heart skipped a beat and I gave Fonda a gentle kick under the table. *"We are going! Didn't you hear him call our names?"* I confidently declared to her as a bolt of electricity seemed to jolt through my body. Strangely, it seemed so obvious. It was settled, our destiny was set! Of course, everything had led to this!

It takes perception and faith to embrace something that you sense is right when uncertainty challenges you intellectually. Many people operate by fear and reject the unknown, thus missing the privilege of walking by faith. The inner gut feeling can all too easily be dismissed. It seemed to me that this decision to go to England was *right*, not because of reasoning it to be so, but because of an inner perception I believed was the nudging of God. I never waivered from acting on this decision.

After the meeting, I made my way to the front of the dining room to boldly ask the general manager what I needed to do to be considered as part of the British administrative staff. Politely, he directed me to the newly formed company's international headquarters in Boston.

As Fonda and I drove through Albany and the Berkshire Mountains to our home that evening we opened the car windows to declare our praises to the Lord with raucous shouts of victory! I'm sure our sound to heaven got the attention of heavenly hosts!

I wasted no time calling the organization's international CEO to arrange that infamous interview. Our meeting was scheduled in the penthouse suites at the top of the beautiful Prudential Building in downtown Boston; the skin-care company being a subsidiary of another large corporation. I took Fonda with me to the interview promoting her as my administrative assistant in the newly formed company in England. This made a great deal of sense to me. I hoped that my success with the company qualified me for an executive position. Had I not been so young and naive perhaps I would never have been so presumptive. Or perhaps, as I believe, this idea was the Lord's prompting.

MEETING THE EXECS   The top executive officers of the two organizations wined and dined us like royalty in the penthouse dining room while a fashion show provided delightful entertainment. I had captured a captive audience and they seemed to be mesmerized by my story. Fonda and I were having the time of our lives!

The gentlemen listened attentively to hear how I had put Maine and Massachusetts on the map. We stifled back giggles as we were directed to the push-pin map indicating where all the company's consultants were working. It amazed me to see what a great number of push-pins represented my team! For years the company had tried to activate those two regions without success, so my story of building this territory in a few short months intrigued them! They were so far above the rank of the lowly grassroots skin-care consultant that they had never actually observed or participated in a class. Although they may have been amused by it all, I truly believe it was a divine opportunity. Then and there I conducted a genuine skincare class with style and verve, as I had done many times before only this time it was before a group of powerful executive gentlemen rather than a roomful of ladies! What great fun it was!

Since Fonda and I rarely got a chance to shop in Boston, after spending several hours at the interview we politely excused ourselves so we could dash to Filene's Department Store's renowned bargain basement in search of a few bargains. Mr. Browning, CEO of the international division, escorted us to the Prudential building's plaza, pointing us in the direction of the subway. Before we parted company, however, he told me that he was extremely impressed with my contribution to the company and that he would do everything in his power to see to it that details could be arranged for me to go as their newest executive director!

My faith was so strong that those *details* would all be worked out that I scarcely heard him caution, *"I must tell you, Marjorie, that for you to acquire the necessary working papers it will be our job to convince the powers that be in England that no one in their country would be qualified to perform this job. I shall contact you as soon as we have a response. It is unlikely, however, that you will get the approval."*

I nodded, already wondering what treasures Fonda and I would unearth in our bargain hunt in downtown Boston! Despite Mr. Browning's doubts, I felt certain that even though the odds were against me, I would soon be embracing a new chapter in England!

His probing question surely gave food for thought as we stood on the plaza steps about to part company. *"I am curious,"* he queried, *"What is your secret, Marjorie, to have broken all sales records in the history of this company?"*

"Mr. Browning", I began as I looked him directly in the eye, *"I believe in the power of prayer."*

Although my response was probably not what he expected, in the months to come he would most definitely see the results of those prayers. I wouldn't see him again until David and I boarded the company's private jet in Boston to embark upon our exciting victory flight to England

CHAPTER 6

ENGLAND ASSIGNMENT

The weeks came and went following that infamous interview in Boston. I never doubted for a minute that my company would send me to England. I expected to get the green light from Mr. Browning any day! I was so convinced that we would be going soon that I slowed down booking *'classes'* to get ready. My income nose-dived. Once again my situation became critical.

BIRTHING   The conception and birthing of my vision to go to England reminds me of the natural birthing process. My vision was *conceived* that evening in Albany at the rah-rah meeting when I heard about the newly formed London branch of my company. I sensed that this was an open door for which the Lord would give me the faith to pursue. Faith comes by hearing and I had heard something that caused my spirit to leap within me. It had been a divine moment.

"Yes Lord, I will go!

Mary was quick to respond to the angel that she would be willing to birth the Savior of the world, by humbly responding with an unequivocal *"Yes!...May your Word to me be fulfilled"* (Luke 1:38)! She received the Vision in obedience by speaking the Word.

For a natural birth to occur there is an inevitable wait following the conception. Under the right conditions the baby grows until it is too big for the womb and must be birthed. There is nothing one can do to hasten the WAIT! Time passes. Impatience is a constant reminder of that waiting heart's desire! Things become uncomfortable; desire becomes more intense. The pressure seems insurmountable!

As the seed grows it becomes harder to carry. It is so hard to wait for that birth. Perfect timing is necessary. A birth too soon or too late may bring dire consequences. Just before one's vision is actually manifested the pressure becomes very intense. The grace for waiting just doesn't seem to be there any longer. But just as it is darkest immediately before the dawn, so is the pain most severe just before the birth. Finally the contractions begin with accompanying pain coming at regular intervals. Although unpleasant, these pains are not intolerable. Then comes that brief *transition* period in the natural between normal contractions and delivery. Transition is when the pain becomes intense and the mother is totally absorbed in delivering. The doctor tells her not to push just yet, but it is all she can think about.

Now it was time for my vision to be birthed. If I didn't get the go ahead soon I would have to put aside my hopes and concentrate on rebuilding my clientele and business. There were demands that I had put off which would need my attention if I were not going to England. It was time to hear that my working papers had been approved. I felt such an urgency! My faith and prayers would require me to *'bear down'* and *'push'*!

PERSISTENCE AND PERSEVERENCE   Following that infamous meeting in Boston with Mr. Browning and his associates the Lord graced me with patience. And faith. I believed I was destined to be sent to England. It would glorify the Lord. This would require persistence and perseverance. I had to learn to quiet myself and let the Lord bring the vision to pass in His way.

Perseverance is often the backbone of success! Read these words from the past which recognize this fact:

"When you get to the end of your rope, hang on" (Franklin D. Roosevelt).

"By perseverance the snail reached the ark" (Charles Spurgeon).

"Perseverance is the secret of all triumphs!" (Victor Hugo).

I am reminded of the story of the poor widow with a desperate need. She knew her need could only be met by the judge avenging her. She couldn't meet her need by herself. She persevered. She never gave up, even though the ungodly judge did not grant her desire in a timely fashion. I love her persistence! Finally the judge granted her petition just to be rid of her. The Word says our God *"will avenge His elect speedily"*, unlike the judge's carelessly slow response; *"For some time he refused"* (Luke 18:1-4). But like the widow woman, I needed my God to bring it to pass; to come to my defense! He was my only resource!

The enemy will try to rob us of our destiny by bringing obstacles and delays. When that occurs it is time to put on our spiritual armor and fight the spiritual forces opposing our vision. It was time to break down the walls of opposition, the gates of delay! I couldn't wait any longer!

Prayer would be the answer! On a Friday night I drove to the Bible college to meet with one of the *'King's daughters'* to join me in prayer. We cried out to God, declaring the Word and reminding Him of His promises. We came against evil forces and delay that were trying to hinder God's plan. We labored in prayer, birthing that vision! We prayed long into the night until we felt a breakthrough, forgetting all about time.

As that wintry night was becoming morning I approached the parking lot to find my car buried in ice and snow! Unknowingly, our prayer vigil had been accompanied by a ferocious snow storm! A raging blizzard had interrupted the silence of the night! Even natural weather conditions were fighting against me! But God was on my side! After scraping snow and ice off my windshield I headed to the main road beyond the parking lot concerned about driving home in such dangerous conditions. Although I only encountered one vehicle on the trip to my home in a nearby town, miraculously that car slowly drove directly ahead of me all the way to my doorstep perfectly lighting my way with his bright headlights! I have always been convinced that I was escorted safely home that night by an angel!

Some time earlier I had faced a similar situation. While driving home through the Berkshire Mountains from Maine to Massachusetts I found myself in a ferocious blizzard! It was dark. It was freezing cold! I couldn't discern the highway from the surrounding blinding white landscape! I was terrified. As I called upon the Lord I became encapsulated in a cocoon-tunnel of soft light all the way home. Although there was white-white snow all around me, I could see clearly and was ushered safely home. It was super-natural! I knew that the Lord had assigned an angel to come to my aid.

Early the following Monday morning Mr. Browning called, *"You must have been in your prayer closet, Marjorie"!* The call I had been waiting for came at last! Mr. Browning had begun to take my prayers seriously. *"Just when it looked as if your papers were being denied, somehow they were strangely accepted. How soon can you be ready?"*

A *suddenly* had just occurred! Hindering spirits also known as a *'blizzard'* and *'delay'* had tried to stop my destiny, but ultimately God won the victory! Warfare prayers had touched heaven and broken through!!! I finally had my green light!

PREPARATIONS   The feathers begin to fly! A semi-truck arrived to pack up my houseful of belongings placing them on a piggy-back carrier to be shipped to England. There was one last company banquet in Albany, NY in which I would be introduced as the newly appointed executive director for our new Great Britain start-up enterprise. It was a wonderful opportunity to give God the glory for my achievements.

I told the ladies, *"I wish I had a 'rubber stamp formula' that you could take home with you to replicate, assuring your own success. What I have to offer is my story. My success was not a result of my past experience, education or charisma. I don't have any particular sales secrets either. My desperate dilemma offered no solutions but to commit my way to the Lord".* They heard my story; that I had found myself almost destitute in a town deep in the throes of a recession, divorced with rebellious children. I told them about the prayer-that-changed-everything and the skin-care products Christmas gift. I told them about committing my override to sponsor the bible school team and that my *downline* caught the vision, too; and a portion of each of their sales supported that cause, too.

"I recruited my friend in Maine and she also caught the vision, which put her territory on the map, as well. Because of my mustard seed faith, God showed me favor and brought increase. This is really His success story!"

They heard how prayer changed things in my life as it could in theirs, too. Tears were flowing freely as ladies were touched with hope for their own situations. Many of the ladies were recording my talk. Only eternity will reveal the complete results of how my story affected lives.

A day or two before we were to leave the country, David's father called demanding to take him to Maine during his school's spring break. Ordinarily I would have been stressed by his call, but this time I felt rather smug as I responded to his bullying, *"I am sorry to say that David will not be here next week. We are flying to London on a private jet where I am to be the featured speaker at my company's opening at the new Hilton. It's quite a marvelous opportunity for David and he is quite excited about it!"*

It was a moment of justice after being put down before the children so often. How many times had he told the children that I would never find work or amount to anything! God had vindicated me just as He had promised according to His Word and it felt really good! Praise be to the Lord! *"It is mine to avenge; I will repay"* (Rom. 12:19), says the Lord.

At last the infamous day arrived in which David and I were onboard the private company Lear jet flying to our new Cinderella-story life in England; the very place I had been sending monthly support to our church team! The company president and general manager flew with us. And, of course, dear Fonda with her little girl came along not as a company employee, but as David's nanny. David, now a seven year old boy obsessed with airplanes, was ecstatic checking out the controls in the cockpit alongside the pilot! We bypassed customs. I was given a handsome, new aqua automobile fashioned by Volkswagen just for our company's executives. Learning to drive on the wrong side of the road presented a few challenges, but I always felt like a princess in my shiny, new chariot. This was what having God's favor felt like!

WE ARRIVE AT LAST!   We found a lovely cottage to rent on the outskirts of a quaint little village in Essex county. Since our new life style provided sweet solitude for frequent times of prayer, the name of the village, 'Chapel', seemed strangely appropriate, if not prophetic! In many ways it was a chapel experience. It was surely a time of refreshment from the tedious season of difficulty and struggle from which I had just emerged. In reality the glamour of my executive position in the cosmetic company was a disguise for the inward life of prayer to which my Lord had called me. All this in a remote little village called 'Chapel'.

Surrounding our cottage were sheep farms. The bleating of the lambs was clearly audible in the background whenever we were outside. This was a constant reminder to me of my own frequent cries to my Good Shepherd and my utter dependency upon Him. Often David and I would go walking in the countryside, finding a comfortable grassy place to rest awhile to observe those captivating sheep. How like those sheep we were; so in need of guidance, yet so easily frightened! Sometimes one of the sheep would venture off on his own away from the flock. I was reminded of the Biblical shepherd's 'crook'. By placing that special crook around the lamb's neck the shepherd could gently pull him back to the fold. He would often carry that wayward or weary lamb next to His bosom where it would feel the security and safety of his Shepherd. I am so very thankful that the tender, loving kindness of my gentle Good Shepherd never allowed me to become too far removed from Him and the flock in spite of my own strong will.

DAVID'S FAITH   David had been taking a great interest in horses and began asking me if I would buy him one. I was not in a position to care for a horse, but David was persistent! I suppose I brushed him off suggesting that he might pray about it. The neighbor behind our garden had purchased a horse shortly before we moved in. Unknown to any of us, the mare had been pregnant when the neighbors purchased her. To our surprise, one morning we awoke to the most cunning wobbly-legged roan-colored colt right on the other side of our garden fence. David spent much time enjoying *'his'* new horse. The joy that colt brought him was a constant reminder to me of God's faithfulness, even to a little child! And my son was learning to bring his requests to the Lord.

DAVID'S PONY

The handsome salary I had agreed to while still in the States no longer appeared so handsome leaving me with a compromised income once again. It seemed that the Lord loved watching me walk by faith! So with my still unrented house in the States demanding regular mortgage payments, we still had to practice frugality. This provided a marvelous opportunity to teach young David the joy of trusting God for our provisions.

Just as he had been wishing for a horse, so had he wanted a guitar. Our home had always housed a grand piano at center stage. Music had been an important feature of our home life, especially for David. Whether a piano concerto or a simple praise chorus, my piano playing had always drawn him out of the woodwork like a magnet to be close to the music. I hated disappointing him by saying that there was no money just now for a guitar. On his own, however, David was learning the power of his prayers and began tenaciously petitioning the Lord himself!

We immediately started attending church services with the British team I had been supporting on my business override. Now, it seemed, was their turn to bless us. The church was mostly made up of young single bible school students, fervent and passionate about their faith. One Sunday morning as we pulled into the church parking lot one of the young ladies virtually ran to our car to greet us! She had been waiting expectantly for us. I shall never forget her words, punctuated with that pristine English accent:

"Da–veed", Her words were crisp, but filled with excitement, *"The Lord has laid it upon my 'haawt' to geeve my 'gee–taw' to you!"*

With that she handed David what he was certain was the most beautiful guitar ever! His bright, blue eyes danced with joy and he was all a-wiggle! He was overwhelmed with Janey's kind generosity! This began his lifelong love affair with the guitar. In time, he became an extraordinary guitarist and quite an anointed musician in his church. The Lord so graciously started David's musical experience through his own answered prayer.

YOUNG DAVID WAS DESTINED TO BECOME A MASTER GUITARIST

My company's headquarters in Great Britain were in London, about an hour's train ride away. My work involved recruiting new skin care consultants, introducing the product and conducting meetings in elegant hotels around the area, but often I could work at home. This kept me close to David which was indeed a Godsend. Fonda was there to keep house and look after him when business took me away. It was an ideal arrangement.

One specific skin-care class stands out in my mind. The hostess had set up my display area on a table at the front of her parlor with her guests conveniently sitting in front of me. It was an intimate gathering; we were quite close to one another. We were close enough that I observed nearly all the ladies had quite a surplus of facial hair! To be honest, they wore beards! Maybe there was something in the water...! Although this was somewhat distracting in a skin care class, it wasn't nearly as distracting as the goings-on directly behind me. No more than just a couple of feet away perched a large cage housing several ferrets! Yes, you read it correctly! *Ferrets!* Active ferrets! I shouldn't confess it, but I have always had a phobia about rodents. They really, really scare me! It was only by the grace of God that I got through that evening, but never forgot the dreadful sound of those ferrets in their cage and their peculiar rapid hunching movements going on right behind me! And those beards!

THE FASHION SHOW   My first important business breakthrough came through a very effeminate boutique owner. When Fonda and I showed up at his shop one afternoon he began telling us stories of his experiences, some of which were unbelievably humorous. In those days we were frequently hearing words or phrases typically British, yet unfamiliar to us. Sometimes these phrases seemed absolutely hilarious to our ears! I shall always remember the phrase he used in describing a situation he found very funny. As he recalled the episode he could barely contain himself. *"It was so hilarious"*, he giggled, *"I nearly 'cropped' my rompers!"* It took me a minute to decipher his strong Cockney accent to understand what he actually meant. It seemed like such a strange expression! Once we understood, Fonda and I couldn't get out of there fast enough to howl with embarrassed laughter!

The boutique owner contracted with me to speak and demonstrate product at his upcoming spring fashion show in a neighboring village. We were ecstatic about this initial opportunity, counting the days until the show. The morning of the fashion show I awoke with a nasty case of laryngitis—-so severe that the only trace left of my voice was a tiny, hoarse rattle! There was nothing to do but to enlist Fonda's assistance, in spite of her protests. She would have to do the presentation! There was no other option! Reluctantly, she agreed. I would whisper to her what to say while she did the makeover on me, seated in front of her facing the audience. Obviously, this made a very unorthodox presentation. The polite British ladies, however, gave us no indication whatsoever that they thought there was anything out of the ordinary in this demonstration!

Somehow we managed to get through the presentation with straight faces. Stifling frequent urges to giggle we took our seats in the audience to watch the fashion show. The boutique owner used his own customers as the models, a diverse collection of ladies of various shapes and ages. This proved to be quite acceptable to the British audience. Fonda and I were simply astounded as we watched the first model parade down the cat-walk——scantily dressed in matching turquoise girdle and bra! This model was unashamedly overweight. Rolls of fat circled her ample girth hanging over her girdle like soft bread dough, quivering with each step she took! As the fashion show progressed she would reappear periodically, modeling one costume after yet another. Every time she made a fresh appearance Fonda and I stifled our giggles as the image of her previously parading down the cat-walk wearing those colorful under garments was still all too vivid!

We learned something that night about the British sense of humor or perhaps what we considered to be the lack of it!

FLAT TIRE   Eventually the fashion show ended. We packed up our pots of creams being the last to leave. After quite an entertaining evening we approached my lovely new company automobile discovering in horror that *a rear tire was flat!* All the fashion show guests had gone home. The village was quiet as a tomb! When we opened the 'boot', as the trunk is called in England, we couldn't find the spare tire!

Stupidly, I had never thought to locate it earlier. Now we were really in trouble. In our despair, we noticed a stereotype English gentleman in his typical London fog trench coat approaching us from a couple of blocks away. Since my laryngitis made my voice inaudible I had to whisper to Fonda, *"You will just have to ask the gentleman for help. It's our only option!"*

Fonda's feeble request to him will forever ring in my ears, *"Sir,"* She feebly began, *"Could you kindly help us find our spare tire?"*

Suddenly, we both felt very foolish and vulnerable. Perhaps it was our elegant attire, perhaps the late hour, or just our silly expressions, but his poignant reply startled us! *"Av you liiii-dies beeeen to the pub? Would you care to come to my flat for a sherry, or a little smoke?'"*

After we explained our situation he called a cab for us to get home to our children behaving in a most gentlemanly and respectful way. We profusely thanked him, climbed into our cab and laughed all the way home.

FONDA AND JOLIE

Fonda and I always celebrated our birthdays together since they are only a week apart; that memorable day was actually my birthday. What an outrageous celebration we had. God certainly entertained us that evening by giving us a celebration we could have never imagined!

There were many occasions in which we found ourselves overcome with the hilarity of our situation. We often laughed till our sides felt like bursting. It surely was God's anecdote for the underlying difficult situations we were both experiencing. I am convinced that the Lord has a keen sense of humor! *"Laughter does good like a medicine"* (Prov. 17:22 KJV).

BACK TO THE STATES   The months flew by. This American based cosmetic company was being received well in Great Britain. I had recruited many consultants successfully. I had become quite the career woman, something I never imagined in my earlier days as a house-wife. The Lord was stretching me and molding me, this lump of yielded clay in His hands. Our bible school team became our church family. We were becoming very close to them as our hearts were being knit together in God's love!

My tri-plex home back in Massachusetts which had been left hastily in the hands of a real estate agency remained unrented after many months. The agency had not found suitable tenants in all that time. I had a dilemma on my hands. The hefty mortgage payments were squeezing me financially. I began to seek God's guidance for His wisdom and answers. Moving to England protected David from the constant threat of having his dad take him back to Maine with his brother and sister. But as long as I was in England I wouldn't see Aria and Tim. I ached for them! I was torn.

As I sought the Lord's voice and guidance I learned about the Old Testament Urim and Thummim. The Scriptures do not tell us in abso-lute detail what they were, but it is generally agreed that the Urim and the Thummim were two stones worn on the ephod or in a pocket of the prophet. When the man of God needed to obtain specific direction from God, he would respond with a *yes* or a *no* through the Urim or

Thummim. If the Urim glowed the answer was *yes* and if the Thummim glowed the answer was *no*. If neither glowed that meant that that God was not giving an answer at that time.

1 Samuel 23:9-11 illustrates: *"When David knew Saul had secretly planned evil against him he said to Abiathar the priest, 'Bring the ephod here.' Then David said, 'O Lord God of Israel, Your servant has certainly heard that Saul seeks to come to Keilah to destroy the city because of me. Will the man of Keilah deliver me up into his hand? Will Saul come down, as Your servant has heard? O Lord God of Israel, I beg of you, tell Your servant.' And the Lord said, 'He will come down.' "*

God answered David with a Urim in the ephod. And so in the Old Testament there was this means of receiving a *yes* or *no* answer from God. You might ask, *"Where is it today then?"* It is in our heart, our soul, our spirit. God has placed within each of us a spiritual Urim and Thummim, a revelation that will cause us to receive a *"yes"* or a *"no"* answer. These things have become spiritual in the New Covenant, so in a sense we still have a Urim and a Thummim.

We can come to God in prayer still with that kind of question. *"Lord, must I do this?"* And the answer will come up from within your spirit as a, *'yes, yes,'* or a *'no way.'* We will sense it in our spirit. We will feel it as a surge which says, *"Yes, it is good, do it."* Or we will feel a check in our spirit. It is a gut feeling producing peace. God is speaking to us through our spirit.

Gradually I began to sense that the Lord would have me return to Massachusetts, that this time in England had been a reprieve, a setting apart for refreshment, but not for long term as I had originally thought. I trusted His promise to *'give wisdom liberally'* to all those who ask for it. My employer had graciously offered to purchase my house in Massachusetts should I decide to stay in England, but after much prayer I decided to deny the company's offer thinking that it would put me under undue bondage to them. My employer thanked me for getting their company launched in Great Britain and for enlisting and training such a great group of skin-care consultants. They generously provided the return airfare for David and me and shipped my household belongings home, as well. We scheduled our flight back from London to New York La Guardia airport.

MIRACLE STAND-BY SEATS   Fonda had come to Great Britain as David's nanny, not as a company employee. With our finances so tight, purchasing Fonda and Jolie's return airfare was beyond our combined means. But never mind. We knew the Lord would make a way as we had seen Him do so often previously in other situations. We began trusting and thanking Him for stand-by tickets for Fonda and Jolie. From our little cottage prayer closet in our remote English village our prayer requests seemed quite reasonable and logical. With childlike faith we made our specific requests known to Him. We petitioned:

"Precious Lord Jesus, You have been faithful to generously provide for every step of our journey. You have been faithful to keep Your Word which tells us that 'You supply all our needs'. You are a good God, always looking after us. You have shown us undeserved favor again and again. Fonda and Jolie need stand-by tickets on the same flight as David and I".

We continued with praises to the skies and truly believed He would answer. *"Thank you, Lord, for providing those seats!"*

Reminding Him of His Word, we added one more thing. *"Your Word says 'You have not because you ask not' ".* (James 4:2). *There is nothing too hard for you, lovely Jesus, so we are asking, 'Will you please arrange for those seats to be adjoining so we might sit together?' "* When we arrived at the crowded London air terminal, however, we began to realize the irrationality of our petitions

When we requested two stand-by tickets preferably adjoining the previously purchased tickets for David and me, we were met with scorn and annoyance.

"That will be highly impossible!" The ticket agent snapped. *"There are many folks in this crowded terminal that have been waiting for those*

stand-by seats much longer than you. Your expectations are unreasonable, but we will do what we can. It is most unlikely."

By this time I had gotten quite used to ignoring the word *impossible*, since the Lord had so many times turned the impossible into possible for me, having delivered me out of one impossible situation after another. The four of us settled into the terminal's waiting area to see just how the Lord would resolve His two very dependent handmaiden's dilemma this time. We amused the children while praising the Lord for His faithfulness.

We had come this far by faith, as the old song goes, *"Trusting in the Lord!"* Surely He would not fail us now. Finally it was boarding time. David and I lingered back as long as possible before boarding, still trusting for Fonda and Jolie's stand-by seats. Just when it seemed as if they would not be forthcoming, the ticket agent hastily trotted our way, waving those two coveted tickets in his hand! Someone had pulled some strings at zero hour and the necessary tickets became available just in time! As we climbed aboard the mighty 747 jet we examined the tickets for our seating designations. Our seats indeed were adjoining just as we had requested! We continued our journey rejoicing in the power of prayer and God's favor over us yet again!

ANGELS   Our flight arrived at LaGuardia in the early evening, too late for us to connect with a bus traveling to Pittsfield. That meant that we would have to spend the night in New York. With our funds so limited and New York hotel rates so high we sought the Lord for our provision for the night. Fonda and I, our two children and our various pieces of unmatched luggage became a commanding little parade as we marched through the terminal to settle into our tidy group of adjoining seats. The children were instructed to behave. Fonda and I knew just what to do. We thanked the Lord for His faithfulness once again and waited for Him to provide a place for us to sleep that night. We declared His faithful promises knowing He would provide. We waited and waited. A long time. I guess the Lord was checking to see if we really would trust Him.

We must have made quite an impression on one very kind ticket agent who had been keeping his eye on us. When his shift was over he made his way to me, *"Ma'am, do you have a place to stay tonight?"* he asked. I had not told anyone about needing a room, but answered him in the affirmative. *"Follow me",* he directed as we obediently marched behind him, single-file like well-trained soldiers. Following his orders we boarded a shuttle to a *'Riviera Hotel'* along with passengers from Italia Airlines who had missed a connecting flight. Shortly we reached our destination picking up our room keys at the desk. Exhausted from our travels, nothing could have looked more appealing to us than those freshly made beds with their crisp, pristine sheets. We rejoiced at the favor the Lord had once again shown us by jumping on those beds like acrobats, turning our beds into praise trampolines making our own special praise dances to Him!!

We slept very well that night!

The next morning would find us refreshed ready for the last leg of our journey. The kindly bellman that helped us with our luggage seemed to have taken us on as his special assignment. After I had checked out of the hotel he ushered our little party to the hotel's covered portico proudly announcing that he knew just the right taxi to escort us to the bus station. Several taxis came and went. I began to be concerned that we might miss our bus, but he assured me that waiting for his *'special cab'* would be worth the wait. We were patient a little longer.

Eventually a metallic red, very unorthodox Cadillac *taxi* pulled up to the curb as the driver ushered us inside. The cab driver was an immense black man with a scarred face and a mouth that seemed to be facing sideways instead of straight ahead. He was a giant of a man! We took our seats, the children and Fonda in the back and me in the official front passenger seat. Our sweet little bellhop, having accomplished his mission, happily waved us on with a broad smile on his face! I admit that I was a little apprehensive at the uniqueness of this situation, especially since I could NOT see the word *'Taxi'* anywhere on this vehicle!

We hadn't gone very far when the cab driver began to tell us his story: He had been a semi-truck driver for years until a serious highway accident left him severely injured and completely blind in both eyes. Somewhat alarming news considering he was our driver! He told us that his wife had to go to work to support his family of five girls and he stayed home every day with his four-year old. Every day his little girl would tell him, *"Don't worry, Daddy, Jesus will heal your eyes."*

After many months he got his miracle! He was sitting on the sofa with his little girl as she repeated her mantra to him again, *"Don't worry, Daddy, Jesus will heal your eyes."* As he glanced up from where they were seated his eyes perfectly focused on the wall clock. It was three o'clock. His vision SUDDENLY had been completely restored, just as his young daughter's faith had prophesied! Oh! To have child-like faith! Then, he began his prophetic message for us. He held a captive audience. *"I don't know what kind of a situation you are facing."* The situation we faced was overwhelming. I owned a house that needed to be sold, I had no job, we had no savings, nor did we have a place to stay once we returned to Massachusetts. In addition, I was certain that David's father would begin the war to gain total custody of him. Our cab driver continued with great fervor! He was under a strong anointing! *"I am here to tell you that Jesus is big enough to meet whatever challenge you may be facing. Put your trust in Him and He will surely see you through. If He can do it for me He will do it for you."*

He told us how he got a job as a cab driver, his wife was able to quit her job and his injuries were all healed by the grace of God. His powerful testimony of the Lord's goodness and faithfulness was exactly what we needed to encourage and strengthen our own faith! He became our faith booster-shot! By the time we actually arrived at the bus depot we were all in tears. That cherry red cab was filled with the electric presence of the Holy Spirit bubbling like a fountain all over us! We piled out of the cab, our luggage in tow, hugged our driver and one another and boarded our waiting bus.

Fonda and I were certain that the two ticket agents, the bellhop and the cabdriver were all angels sent to guide us back to Massachusetts with the Lord's blessings and favor upon us.

We boarded our bus wondering what awaited us back in Massachusetts.

CHAPTER 7

HIS SECRET DWELLING PLACE

MY WORD FROM THE LORD   After deciding to return to the States I sought the Lord to give me a word which would guide me in my new venture. I wanted encouragement to satisfy the anxiety I was feeling. Knowing I was returning to face a battle, I needed a positive word promising victory. When the words from scripture nearly jumped off the page, I knew the Lord was directly speaking to me; I had received a *Rhema* word! But instead of promising victory, He implied the days ahead were going to be tough. Those words were not what I was hoping to hear: *"Darkness is His secret dwelling place!"* (Ps.18:10 KJV).

Had I not heard Him correctly when I thought He was leading me to return to the States? My real estate situation at home required my direct attention. I understood that to mean it would be prudent for me to return. My fairy tale experience in the land of castles, princes, and princesses had come to an end. It had served its purpose in my life. I would not waiver now! *"A double-minded man (or woman) is unstable in all his (or her) ways"* (James 1:8 KJV).

Once I had made my decision I would not look back. I had heard His voice. I would return home without regrets or fear.

The darkness. His secret dwelling place was a place He would lovingly lead me. I was growing up in Him. It was time for my walk of faith to deepen and develop strong roots. I would need strong roots for what He had ahead for me. I nestled close to His bosom and by His grace, praised Him. His word says to *"...put on a garment of praise instead of a spirit of despair"* (Is. 61:3).

I learned that praising the Lord was the best anecdote for feeling overwhelmed. The joy of the Lord is as close as deciding to offer Him the sacrifice of praise. I could choose to praise Him. My mood would lift, my spirits rise and the joy of the Lord would become my strength! The Word speaks of offering up a *sacrifice of praise*. Yes, it was a sacrifice. Nothing in me FELT like praising Him! It is easy to trust the Lord when all is well. But it was in the dark places that I learned victory comes in offering the sacrifice of praise whether I felt His presence or not; when everything around me was unresolved and grim. When even His presence seemed remote I could choose to believe and declare His Word.

"For we know that in all things God works for the good of those who love Him, who have been called according to His purpose" (Rom. 8:28).

"The righteous person may have many troubles, but the Lord delivers him from them ALL!" (Ps. 34:19).

"What the enemy meant for evil the Lord turns for good" (Gen. 50:20 KJV).

"You will surely recover everything that was taken from you!" (1 Sam. 30:8 KJV).

"Everyone who has left houses or brothers or sisters or father or mother or wife or children or lands for My name's sake, shall receive a hundredfold in this life and inherit eternal life!" (Matt. 19:29 KJV).

The classroom God was about to use to teach me to depend fully on Him rather than on my soulish emotions was a *night season*. True to His word, as soon as I set foot back on American soil, that door to the *night season* of His darkness began to appear. God, who created darkness as well as light, dwells in both places. Nighttime is a time in which there is no light. So my natural vision and resources, my logic, and reasoning would be of no use.

My situation was bleak. When I left for England I had put my home in the hands of a realtor. Because he failed to rent the property the entire time I was away the mounting unpaid mortgage payments were staggering. Because of an unexpected shipping strike on the British docks, my furniture and belongings were still in England. There was no telling when they would be shipped home. It would be weeks. I didn't have the money to pay a first and last month's rent plus a deposit on a place to live. Worst, I knew it would be only a matter of time before David's father would be pressing to gain custody of him. In the natural, I was no match for his crafty ways or the skillful lawyers his resources could afford. This loomed heavily over my head knowing how devastating it would be for both David and me if that should happen.

I had barely set foot on the ground back in Massachusetts when my sensitive skin developed an allergic reaction to the skincare products I had been promoting. I believed it was a sign that a door had closed. I would no longer even be able to sell the product. The security of the salary I had earned in England was behind me; nothing was certain and I faced a mountain of bills from unpaid mortgage payments.

I learned the meaning of 'Darkness is His secret dwelling place' (Ps. 18:10). I began to discover the Lord in a dark place where my situation was nothing short of overwhelming, sometimes downright terrifying! How could I cope with all those responsibilities; the financial difficulties, the demonic attacks, frequent ferocious headaches, the constant heartache of losing Aria and Tim, the threat of losing David? Yet, even in the darkest night, God had placed twinkling gems of light called 'stars' just to remind me to have hope; that God is still there. And He comforted me through my darkest hours.

TREASURES OF DARKNESS   As my faith grew I learned to trust Jesus more. He was always there, comforting me and enveloping me with the satisfying love that only He can give. My praises began to replace anxiety. His gift to me was faith, wrapped in invisible waves of love. He patiently waited for me to reach out to Him. What solace and comfort I would find when I would retreat into His presence! There would be difficulties to face, but my God who had been so faithful to me in the past would surely see me through with victory as long as I put my trust in Him. I had to put fear behind me and walk bravely in faith. I was learning that *faith is the currency of heaven.*

The treasures I discovered during that dark season dug out a greater capacity for Him in my life which I would not trade for anything. I am reminded of a simple poem by Robert Browning Hamilton that loudly speaks of the work darkness or sorrow can accomplish in one's life, as it certainly did in my own:

> *I walked a mile with Pleasure;*
> *She chattered all the way;*
> *But left me none the wiser*
> *For all she had to say.*
>
> *I walked a mile with Sorrow,*
> *Ne'er a word said she,*
> *But, oh! The things I learned from her,*
> *When sorrow walked with me.*

Oh! The things I learned from her!! Oh! The things I learned from her!! Indeed His dwelling place was there in the darkness with me. He promised to never leave me nor forsake me. His Word said that even if *"I went into hell He would be there"* (Ps. 139:8 NKJV). I was not alone.

Sometimes I would remember that experience I'd had on that quiet street in Maine some years earlier; my Damascus Road experience. As I remembered tasting the intense love He showered upon me that day I would be refreshed and renewed. He had asked me to *'count the cost'.* Even now many years later, the remembrance of my surrender and being bathed in liquid golden waves of His overwhelming love is still as fresh and moving as if it were yesterday!

I didn't have any answers. It was dark. I began to understand what *'blind faith'* meant as I faced the challenges before me without sight or natural understanding. Lovingly He removed all my natural and comfortable *support systems* to replace them with unshakable faith in Him. My reasoning, my intellect, my emotions were blinded, forcing me to rely totally upon the eyes of my spirit.

Admittedly, I squirmed. I flailed. I pleaded. I cajoled. I tried to figure out what to do. But as the days poured into weeks and then into months, I quieted down. Eventually, I even surrendered my timetable, accepting His. My strong will became quiet. By His grace, I never doubted His love for me. I was His child; He would see me through.

FEAR   I have discovered in life that if I gave an inch to fear it would take a mile. Fear is faith's greatest enemy! Fear can become a stronghold if it is given a place in one's life. This is the clue that fear is not simply an emotion, rather it is a spirit. *"For God has not given us a spirit of fear, but of power and of love and a sound mind"* (2Tim.1:7 KJV).

One of the earliest fears a small child develops is fear of the dark. I recall sitting with my children as their fears of the dark eventually subsided, while cradled in my loving arms they began to trust. It took time. It was a process. Sometimes I would hear my child's tearful, frightened voice calling for me:

'Mommy, I am so afraid of the dark.'

And I would be there to comfort and reassure my child until he or she began to trust.

LEARNING TO TRUST   And so it was with me. I began to trust Him more and more. I learned that sometimes the hardest thing in the world to do is to trust the Lord and surrender my own strong will. Yet, when I truly let go and fully trusted Him what a sweet peace would flood my soul. I would rest.

I recall my childhood swimming lessons. I was a terrible swimming student. I would flail my arms, sputter and kick, kick, kick for all I was worth! But I didn't seem to be very buoyant. As I tried to float in the water I would feel my body begin to sink, then would frantically commence flapping all over again. My instructor would yell, *"No! No! No! You are struggling. Just lie on your back, take a deep breath and let the water support you."* To my surprise, I found that when I eventually let go completely the water *would* support me! By letting go I would be supported! I could relax and float. No more struggle. And it is like that when we learn to trust the Lord. What a resting place it is when we quit our struggle and *"Cast our cares upon Him...*(Ps. 55:22); when we finally are *"...Still and know that He is God"* (Ps. 46:10).

Those dark days were the days of my refining. The bible speaks of God refining us. God cannot trust an untested vessel. At some point in our journey, He will find us ready to be tried by fire. I am reminded that even the most precious diamonds are those that have survived the greatest pressure! The precious metals of gold and silver must endure the refiner's fire. The refiner knows the value of the searing fire. He subjects the metal to the scorching fire, knowing that such fires melt the metal. Only the molten mass releases its alloy or takes perfectly its new form in the mold. The refiner never leaves his crucible, but sits down by it should there be an excessive degree of heat to mar the metal. Too much or too little heat will not produce the finest silver! The refiner skims the last of the dross from the fire as soon as he sees his face reflected. That is when he puts out the fire. *"He shall sit as a refiner and purifier of silver"* (Mal. 3:3). The process may be painful, but He sees us through it. I am so thankful that He watches over us with tender love as He perfects and refines us by fire. Oh! That the Refiner will see Himself reflected in me!

I can bear the refining process knowing that my Refiner will go through it with me; as I yield to Him He will perfect me that I might reflect His very own image.

The Refiner's Fire by Steve Greene:

There burns a fire with sacred heat. He is consuming my soul.
White-hot with holy flame, refining me, making me whole.

I'm learning now to trust His touch, To crave the fire's embrace,
For though my past with sin was etched, His mercies did erase.

Each time His purging cleanses deeper I'm not sure that I'll survive.
Yet the strength in me growing weaker keeps my hungry soul alive.

Chorus:
The Refiner's fire has now become my soul's desire.
Purged and cleansed and purified that the Lord be glorified!

THE ROCK   In the midst of it all, there was a quiet place of shelter, a hiding place, a sanctuary of peace. Oh dear Reader, if you find yourself in a place of darkness where you don't know the way out, there is a solace for you called *The Rock.* *"When my heart is overwhelmed, lead me to the Rock that is higher than I. For you have been a shelter for me, a strong tower from the enemy."* (Ps. 61:2 NKJV). There is a retreat where He is waiting to comfort you, to bring you hope. It is a cleft in the rock that will hide you from the storms of life, from the scary place where there are no answers. Run into that Rock that is higher than you, a strong tower, a refuge. Let God's love wash over your weary, overwhelmed heart and refresh you. It is there in His blessed presence that you will be refreshed. Your overwhelmed heart will find the strength to go on just like I did. I discovered the Rock that was higher than my weakness and I was safe. The Refiner's fire did its work and I became strong.

As I reflect on those days, now many years later, I marvel at God's faithfulness to me. He was there all the time. He brought me to a new level of trust. It was His love for me that took me into that dark place where He dug out a much greater capacity for Himself. God simply used that night season to accomplish His will in me. It was in that secret place that He refined me and drew me closer that I might discover His hidden treasures and revelations of His love. *"I will give you hidden treasures, riches stored in **secret** places, that you may know that I, the Lord, who summons you by name, am God"* (Is. 45:3). I would be forever grateful!

And in His time He resolved every gloomy obstacle that had so fearfully loomed before me.

THE BANKING ANGEL   When we arrived back in Lenox we were invited to stay with gracious friends while things were being sorted out. I shall always be grateful for their warm hospitality. Eventually, we rented an apartment in a classic colonial-style New England home. David didn't seem to mind that his sleeping loft was in reality a luggage closet accessible only by climbing up the headboard of my brass bed. I think he believed that it was a special make-believe secret fort and he enjoyed the special uniqueness of his hide-away bed.

I knew I still had a bank account with a few dollars left in it. One winter morning as I went to the bank to close the account I felt like I was emptying my piggy bank to pull out its last few nickles and dimes. Rent was due, the cupboards were bare and Christmas was right around the corner. I wanted to give a few gifts to the children. When the teller presented the balance of that account I gulped in shock! To the penny, there was exactly enough to meet my needs! My jaw dropped in amazement knowing that I didn't have that much in the account. I sensed the Lord smiling tenderly at me saying that an angel had made a deposit in my account! I joyously skipped home that day with a song in my heart grateful for the creative way the Lord provides.

Fonda and I marched around my unsold home in Pittsfield seven times shouting *"Victory"*, proclaiming the sale of my home as Joshua of old had done to ensure his victory, tearing down the walls of opposition! My white elephant house sold, I paid my unpaid bills and was able to rent a lovely small home near the Bible school. With my usual flair, I went to work making the little cottage charming. I wallpapered a couple of rooms, and made an inviting sun porch out of the enclosed entry, furnishing it with freshly painted antique wicker furniture picked up at flea markets. I put my sewing machine to work and Voila! Stylish new window treatments!

There was an extra room that I rented to a Bible school student. This provided funds to contribute toward the monthly rent. I worked part-time at the Bible college in exchange for David's Christian school tuition. And eventually, I even picked up a few piano students. The divorce had been so traumatic for David that I wanted to provide as much stability as possible for him by being a stay-at-home Mom. By creatively piecing together an income I was able to achieve my goal. I walked everywhere as my meager budget didn't allow for the expense of an automobile. Carrying my weekly laundry in the freezing Massachusetts winter weather to the local laundromat says something about the state of my limited funds. To save a few cents I would carry the damp laundry back home to hang in my cold and damp basement, sometimes taking a few days to dry.

Occasionally my classical piano training became a tent-making skill as the need would arise. A fine five-star restaurant within walking distance of our cozy home in Lenox hired me to play dinner music on a beautiful grand piano in their dimly lit dining room. David would often tag along with me, sitting on the piano bench turning my pages when he wasn't playing with the owner's young son.

CHRISTMAS TOBOGGAN RIDE   Fonda and Jolie lived up the street in a rented apartment and we spent much of our free time together. They were sharing Christmas morning with David and me. David had raced out of the house early to join other kids at the large town hillside to try out his magnificent new toboggan! Conditions were perfect that morning since a fresh blanket of newly fallen snow covered the ground. Aria had come for a Christmas visit but seemed edgy the entire visit. Soon the root of her anxiety became all too obvious!

The serenity of the morning took a startling abrupt turn for the worst by a ferocious, loud pounding at the door! An intense drama was about to unfold! Nothing could have been more shocking than to discover David's father, standing bigger than life with a very black expression on his face, demanding to see *his son*! What a scurrying of activity ensued! Aria, who was part of the conspiracy to *'kidnap'* David to take him back to Maine, grabbed her parka and flew out of our house frantically leading the strangest army of us to the town hill after the lad.

Along the way, Timmy popped out of his dad's waiting get-away car. This being the first time I had seen him since returning from England, I was stunned at how he had grown! He was shouting and crying all at once telling me they were on a mission to take David and never bring him back! Oh! My darling son! And my dear Aria! My beloved children! I hadn't wanted my first meeting with them since my return from England to be like this! What had happened to them? I was in shock! My mother-heart took such a beating!

We were quite a spectacle as we frantically paraded single-file to Toboggan Hill that cold Christmas morning. When we caught up with them the sight was alarming! There they were...on David's bright new Christmas toboggan, he and his dad sitting close behind as they whizzed down the hill with silent velocity. I was desperate and wholly dependent upon the Lord's intervention! How I called upon His mercy and protection! I covered David in prayer with the blood of Jesus taking authority over demonic forces. I tried to remember all the bible verses I could to remind the Lord of His promises to deliver us! My petitions were the passionate, persistent prayers of a desperate mother pleading for her beloved, young son! Indeed his future would be influenced and shaped by how God answered those prayers!

I knew that if David were to be taken back to Maine it would begin an arduous war to retrieve him for which, in my own strength, I was no match. I discovered later that three lawyers had been contracted by David's father to try to gain custody of the boy!

Oddly, after a couple of runs down the hill together father and son parted company.

David joined me as the somewhat dejected trio climbed into the car to make the five-hour return journey back to Maine, *without him!* Oh!

The faithfulness of God! Oh! The power of prayer! That situation was indeed a fork in the road; a battle won in the heavenlies. I shall probably never know exactly what altered the course of events for David's dad, but I know that God intervened! I had experienced the Lord's mercy! If the invisible spirit world could have been made visible that day I believe I would have seen a war waging in which the angelic realm was victorious and the demonic realm took a beating. Shortly after that infamous day of the proposed *kidnapping*, the case was strangely dropped; such a victory for the Kingdom of God!

And so, battles won, we settled into a period of peaceful life in that lovely Berkshire Mountain town. In time, however, it became more and more clear that a change was necessary. There was little opportunity for employment for me there. Because David was about to switch schools to start junior high it was an opportune time to make a move. So after prayerfully considering our options, David and I set out once again for another adventure! This time we would move across the country to Tucson, Arizona. My parents, sister, and her family lived there, so it was a logical choice. Fonda and Jolie tagged along, too, as we had become a spiritual family.

When we arrived in Tucson that suffocating August day, stepping out of the car felt like opening the door to an inferno with desert temperatures soaring to a very dry, scorching 110 degrees! I burst into outrageous laughter wondering what in the world we had done!

We adjusted. The searing hot summer gave way to beautiful, pleasant sunny days all winter long. We were about to build a new life...And God continued to shine His grace upon us!

CHAPTER 8

I'M A DESIGNER!

STABILITY IN TUCSON   The move to Tucson brought stability and order to our lives. One by one the pieces of my broken life began to be put together in a beautiful, yet unpredictable way as the Lord fashioned me further into His likeness. Just like fragile, broken pieces of glass shards, the pieces of my life were being shaped into a one-of-a-kind work of mosaic art; crafted by the Master Himself.

Shortly after our move to Tucson I met and married Darrel, a gentle, kindly man. We would live happily ever after. His kind stability was a resting place for me. Importantly, our marriage would provide needed security and a good role model for David who by this time was a budding pre-teen. My divorce had been so disruptive for him. Sometimes he would have traumatic nightmares of a hideously mean man. I would find him buried under a mountain of covers at the foot of his bed drenched in sweat, where he sought refuge from this monster. It was heartbreaking to watch David silently try to handle his pain alone as he never wanted to burden me with his fear and emotional pain. Even as a young boy he carried a mantle of protectiveness over me.

Some single moms rely on their children to be an emotional crutch for them. I was careful not to put that kind of burden on David, but as a sensitive child, he was well aware of the hardships I had experienced. He often tried to be stronger than his chronological years by shouldering courage he was not mature enough yet to handle. As his mom, this always touched me deeply and I tried to make his life as happy and secure as I could considering the tools I had to work with.

DOORS OPEN   One often selects a second marriage partner to be opposite from the first one. That was true in my case. Darrell was easy-going, relaxed, undemanding, and not at all controlling or possessive as had been my first husband. We bought a pretty home in a new development in Tucson and my designer talents began to blossom as I put my innate design skills to work furnishing and colorizing it.

Darrell was a co-owner of a private post-secondary school. Before long he had me involved in the recruiting process alongside him. Quite a training it was, too, as college admissions was his forte! My previous work in the cosmetic business had begun to hone my entrepreneur side, especially my sales skills. Now I was learning another facet of sales; college admissions. This skill proved to be essential in landing another position in admissions after Darrell sold his interest in the school. Both of us became area directors of admissions with a national airline school which entailed travel throughout the southwest recruiting students.

On one of our trips to Phoenix, I stumbled upon a private interior design school. I had always had an eye for design. Thoughts of that school kept gnawing at me until I finally made an appointment to check it out. I was captivated! Although I had not been thinking of going back to school, I enrolled and became engrossed in my studies.

STEPPING STONES   Many things in my past had been stepping stones to prepare me to for a career in interior design. Childhood summers had always included visits to my grandparents in Idaho where I would spend hours in the furniture store my grandfather owned. I would go from vignette to vignette dusting furniture, imagining which pieces I would have in my own house someday.

Throughout my life I even had many dreams about houses, whether grand or humble, they always left me wanting to go back into my dream to wander through those rooms again and again! My favorite girlhood possession had been a large, handmade dollhouse for which I created endless draperies, rugs, and pieces of furniture out of salvaged scraps of whatever material I could find.

MY BEAUTIFUL HOME IN OREGON SHAPED MY FUTURE

I immersed myself in every detail of the custom home my parents built during my elementary school years, fascinated by the process! Later, when my parents bought a resort on the Oregon coast, my appreciation for good design and architecture was further fueled! Before its conversion into a resort, the property had originally been owned by the Bancroft family, for whom a freeway in Oregon was later named. Nothing had been spared in the exquisite design and detail of that property; a sure contributing factor to my keen interest in fine design and architecture.

I can now easily see the hand of the Lord crafting me into the field of interior design. I had been guided to walk in my destiny. *"I know the plans I have for you, says the Lord; plans to prosper you and not to harm you, to give you hope and a future"* (Jer. 29:11).

Being exposed to the field of architecture was another stepping stone. I wasn't going to let an awkward family move to Seattle the second semester of my senior year dampen my spirits! By landing an afternoon position as a receptionist in an architectural firm I turned a difficult situation into a positive one! This was a big deal for an 18-year-old young lady! Every afternoon after swapping my sensible school shoes for stylish high heels, a long bus ride would deliver me to my new job across town... and my first glimpse of the working world!

My employers had been college classmates. Now in their thirties, they reunited as a blossoming new architectural firm. Their business was finally prosperous enough to hire me as their first employee, so I became a status symbol for them as their front office receptionist. They were like big brothers to me; protective, offering advice for making life choices, and looking out for me in every way they could. When the popular Seattle Seafair festivities came around they insisted on promoting me in the local community competition as a princess. Winning the competition meant riding on a beautiful float through various Seattle neighborhoods, being honored at the Seafair hydrofoil boat races, and numerous community events, including a magnificent and glamorous Cinderella-style ball! Being a princess allowed me to promote the architectural firm that sponsored me. I was exposed to the building industry and watched projects go from a concept to the drawing board, to breaking ground, to the final stage of completion. I loved all aspects of it. But strangely, never considered a career in design until years later when I visited that marvelous design school in Arizona!

Now years later, with newly earned interior design credentials in hand, my brain oozing with design concepts, and possessing a business background I was prepared for my next chapter. What doors would the Lord open for me? Would I eagerly climb on board or shirk back with timidity and insecurity? I have often thought of the well-worn saying, *"Blessings lie at the junction of preparedness and opportunity".*

I was *prepared.* When an *opportunity* came my way would I step out in faith to embrace what God has already prepared for me or would I use the excuse of not being experienced enough, or lack the confidence or faith to move forward? I now wonder what blessings I have forfeited in my life because when an opportunity came knocking I was either not prepared or lacked the confidence to seize it and run with it!

There are times and seasons in our lives. Just as in the natural there are seasons of sowing and reaping, there are seasons of loss and restoration. My natural impatience has been tempered by long, often tedious seasons of waiting on the Lord. As a young woman I failed to value patience; much preferring my impulsive, fly by the seat-of-my-pants nature. For years my mantra was *"Hurry up and wait!"* I have waited, waited, and waited until at last, I would surrender to His perfect timing and His will of molding me into His likeness. It was not easy for one with such an impulsive nature. In time however I have slowly come to value the virtue (yes, virtue!) of patience, discovering it to be a place of rest rather than the place of strife held by its counterpart, impatience, of my younger years! In becoming more patient I learned something about the grace of God, too. I found that His grace is sufficient only if I allow it to be. What a trade-off...His grace for my impatience!

God's timing is everything. As I waited for His opportunity I was reminded of His Word, *"Let us not be weary in well doing for in due season we shall reap if we don't lose heart!"* (Gal, 6:9 NKJV). I guess it was *'due season'* because an opportunity came my way which seemed to meld my background, training, and talents to a tee! God doesn't waste any of our past experiences. This position even drew upon my admission's work background in the private secondary school business. He had fashioned me for this next stepping stone; to become the director of a new private interior design school in Tucson. My duties included finding a property for the school campus, designing it's interior space, recruiting students, teaching the entire curriculum, then placing the graduates in interior design positions in the local marketplace. I was even responsible for marketing the program and developing our logo.

The Lord led me to discover an architecturally *avant-garde* building with just the right character for a design school! We occupied the third floor of a space whose entire northern wall was glass overlooking the beautiful Catalina Mountains. The natural light was perfect, the view spectacular! Doors flew open for me. Students were recruited; motivated and were becoming designers! And I was blooming in my newly found talents, gifts, experience, and training.

DESIGN SCHOOL DIRECTOR   I blossomed in my work. It was demanding, but I seemed well suited for it. Before I could become too comfortable, however, a bomb was about to drop that would change the course of my career! Another chapter was about to unfold! Watch out when things begin to become routine. When I was younger I often said, "*I never want to lead a boring life!*" What power there is in our spoken words; even the things we often say without thinking! Boredom never did find me. Was that mantra of my youth a prophetic utterance?

As soon as things became comfortable it seems that a new challenge would be staring me in the face! God, as my School Master in the school of faith, would present me with one impossibility after the next. And I would learn that He is trustworthy! My life's blueprint for tackling the impossible has been all about trading my insecurity and self-sufficiency for His promises! I could step out into the unknown sea of faith if I knew He was leading me because I believed His Word. He proved Himself faithful every time!

It is amazing what a difference a day can make! One morning, my French History of Furniture lecture was abruptly interrupted when my noticeably shaken employer called me out of the classroom. In his emotionally charged state, he somehow managed to pull himself together enough to express his devastating announcement! His young wife had *tragically and unexpectantly <u>died</u> the previous night!* That shocking news would change the course of my life!

He had purchased this school for his wife. Although I ran the school, she was the owner. He owned numerous other private post-secondary schools throughout the country, but this design school was to be her pet project. With her gone, he no longer had any interest to own or operate it!

He promptly decided to sell the school's curriculum to an established Tucson college. The *'package deal'* included me as the program director complete with a generous salary. The problem was, however, that I hadn't been consulted. I knew that the curriculum carried a written stipulation that it could not legally be sold to another school. As such, I was compelled to refuse the offer much to the anger and verbal abuse of my employer, as well as unfounded threatening letters to me from his attorney. Refusing the offer, however, put me once again in a precarious place of trading the security of the generous salary he offered for the unknown path of faith.

ANOTHER NEW CHALLENGE   Just as all this was occurring, I had a sudden health issue forcing me to stay home for a week of bed rest. God always seems to know how to get my attention! It was during that week that the Lord spoke into my spirit that in my next chapter I would not have an employer! He had gone before me, already fully equipping me to own and operate a school for myself! Imagine that! I had already set up, recruited, taught, and placed design students for my employer. I knew every aspect of the school business! Now He was opening the door for me to open a school of my own! It was uncanny! Why not? This was a startling and somewhat daunting idea; one I had never yet considered. Nonetheless, many logical arguments were shouting in my ear!

"Who me?"

"But I have so little experience!"

"Where will I get the finances? I don't have enough money."

"What if I fail?

"I am no match for the competition!"

The local community college currently offered an interior design degree program. The private college that bought my boss's program was aggressively advertising their new design program. The one I had declined! Both schools offered generous federal student loans and grants, something I was not yet equipped to offer.

Those excuses were all true, but were not the facts! The fact was, *"I can do all things through Christ who strengthens me"* (Phil 4:13). I would squirm and fuss, but in my heart, I knew God was offering me an opportunity to accept a call to faith, but it would take all the courage I could muster! It was a fork in the road in which I could accept as a gift from God, or dismiss in doubt or unbelief. I could be His vessel through which He would lead and guide. I refused to let insecurity or fear of failure deter me. This was a divine opportunity!

I returned to class at the end of the week with a resolve to not only train out the existing students but to begin the process of fulfilling my new vision of starting my own institute of interior design!

The feathers were flying! There were tedious weeks of filling out application papers for my license to operate a school in the state of Arizona. The school from which I had graduated agreed to sell me their well-established curriculum with reasonable monthly payments. The Lord had planted an idea in my head for the ideal facility. It would need to meet local zoning regulations with adequate parking. I began envisioning a beautiful large residence to house my school; a perfect setting to showcase residential design! I pictured a large classroom complete with a design materials lab to house samples of textiles, flooring materials, and furniture catalogs for student projects. Ideally, there would be space for offices, kitchen and snack rooms as well as a student lounge. I wanted a small retail showroom/design firm included in the space so the students could observe the actual work of interior designers right under their noses!

It was a tall order yet one I could not locate. Either I would find a perfect residence that would not have adequate parking, or would have adequate parking and zoning, but have an inadequate building. I was running out of time. What to do? I had been *"Leaning on my own understanding"* rather than *"trusting in the Lord with all my heart"* as the Word instructs (Prov. 3:5). When I finally loosened my grip on finding *my ideal property* my realtor called located a lovely facility which, although not my original idea, did meet my needs quite nicely. I signed a five-year lease and began the process of marketing my new school.

I have found throughout life that it is possible to hang onto something so tightly that it may strangle the process of moving forward. In this case, it simply was not time to realize my ideal residential property as I had envisioned it. It would come in time. I could have waited forever for that dream facility to appear, but there is such a thing as God's perfect timing. Sometimes we must die to our vision. We must submit to God's will and His timing while walking by faith. I was trusting God with all my heart, yet was learning to hang on to my vision loosely so He could shape it and develop it in His timing! *"Submit ourselves under the mighty hand of God and in due season He will raise you up"* (1 Pet. 5:6 KJV). There was *due season* again! I believe He had given me a vision of His idea for what my 'ideal' school facility would be. But it would require a 'stepping stone' facility first. After I put MY desire and vision to rest and let it lie dormant for a season, He would resurrect it *in due season*. In the meantime, I took it by faith, tenaciously trusting the Lord.

Truly, the Lord had directed my footsteps in the selection of this initial site. It was situated on one of Tucson's most visible and highly trafficked intersections in a very charming Southwest- style up-scale shopping facility with ample parking on a cobblestone parking lot. The interior space was perfect! The Lord amply met all my needs; office space, large classroom, and student lab/library space, and a perfect-sized retail design showroom in the front of the space with ideal visibility from the street.

YELLOW PAGE AD   I marvel at how the Lord put everything together to the last detail, often in quite unexpected ways. Before we moved in I met with the yellow page representative who took my written ad to place in the next book. He laughed at me when I told him I hadn't yet come up with a logo but would supply it at our next meeting.

"There won't be a 'next meeting', ma'am," he chuckled, *"We are closing the applications for the next book this week. If you want to have a logo you must give it to me today."*

It was poor timing for my mind to go blank, but the only design symbol I could visualize was the over-used *fleur de lis*. I wanted a unique motif! Over the top! Mine alone! Why was I stuck at only being able to think of that trite, over-used motif? But, rather than have my yellow page ad appear bland without artwork and go unnoticed I reluctantly decided on using *fleur de lis*. Was I *'settling'?* I opted for triteness.

When the agent asked me to draw the symbol as it would appear in the ad, I knew my drawing skills would not allow me to produce something adequate for camera-ready art on such short notice. Not to be defeated, pondering where I might locate an example, I selected my desk copy of Webster's Dictionary. There I found a minute drawing of the classic *fleur de lis,* cutting it out carefully with my penknife. Granted, the example I found was only about one-half-inch high, it sufficed to supply the rep with the necessary artwork. For years whenever I glanced at that desk-top dictionary I would smile knowing that in the 'F' section there would always be a cut-out hole where the *fleur de lis* had once been.

Eventually, I refined that original logo, stylizing it to become more '*chic'.* The symbol I had selected served my business well. I named the design firm '*Fleur de Lis Design'* and my business name became associated with that symbol; a sign of good branding. With a marketing plan in place, the five-year lease signed and sealed and a peace that I was moving in God's will I moved forward in faith.

SHOWROOM ENTRANCE & MY FLEUR DE LIS LOGO

SHOWROOM DISPLAYS

ENTER JUSTIN   Because I had no experience running a retail showroom it was probably a hasty decision to have started this venture in tandem with such a colossal undertaking as opening a private post-secondary school. When Justin bounded into the showroom one afternoon suddenly appearing as if an angel had sent him (which I believe was the case), I began to suspect that the Lord might be bringing me help.

This is what he said: *"I have just moved here from San Francisco where I owned and operated an interior design business and showroom. I was just strolling around today trying to find a place to land while I am searching for my next career move."* I immediately was drawn to Justin's compelling personality.

"It was the logo in your showroom window that compelled me to come in," he continued. *"For seventeen years that was the exact 'Fleur de Lis' I used in my business. I felt like I was coming home!"*

Indeed he was *'coming home'* as he became my showroom manager adding his experience and charm to the mix. Justin agreed to work without a salary for a season while I built up a little revenue. God poured out His favor upon me before I had even called upon Him! *"Before they call I will answer, while they are still speaking I will hear"* (Is. 65:24). How great is our God!!! I was discovering that He was always way ahead of me!

MAGAZINES   In the back of my mind was the continual nagging of how I would acquire enough design magazines for my student projects. There would be many cut and paste class projects calling for pictorial examples from design magazines. I didn't have the money to buy the ample supply that I knew we would need. Just before our first class began I received a phone call from a woman who had seen an ad I had placed to advertise the school. She was an art historian who had been subscribing to *Architectural Digest* as well as other design magazines for years. Her call could not have been more timely or appreciated.

"I have a collection of magazines I would like to donate to your new school if you could come by to pick them up!" she quite generously announced. Later when she escorted me to her garage to pick up her collection my foolish fears were alleviated! What I discovered was beyond my hopes... a thirty-year collection of *Architectural Digest* and other design magazines, all in pristine yearly collections, bound and neatly tied with cord! She became a wonderful resource to the students as she continued to donate magazines as well as offer her beautifully decorated home as a destination for field trips for many classes to come.

I never ran out of magazines. Just when the supply would run low, someone would donate their used collection. I would be always be reminded of God's faithfulness!

START-UP   I needed students, of course. Four students loyally followed me from the school in which I had formerly been the director. They opted to wait for my school to open to complete their training. My limited advertising produced four more students in that "charter" class, two of which were medical professionals, a doctor, and a nurse. And by the grace of God, I started my first month with a profit, a rather remarkable feat in the business world! Nor did I borrow money! What did I know about business? But I had committed my way unto the Lord and He was directing my path. He and I were now in the design business. He was the boss.

Startup expenses were a challenge for me. Initially, I had no idea how everything would fall into place. With my meager budget, I managed to furnish the school and my design studio with elegance and style! Second-hand stores provided individual round wooden tables to tastefully become each student's work station. Each tabletop was painted with its' own individual floral wreath by one of my artistic-students. Old military steel and leather chairs were a second-hand store find. Their shabbiness was hidden under chic floor-length damask chair *dresses* which I tailored for each one. The classroom took on a very stylish aura, perfect for a design school. I placed two French chairs clad in chic ecru-colored damask chair-dresses in front of my old French desk from home, thus elegantly furnishing my office.

What fun it was to find just the right pieces to furnish my showroom, opening design accounts with payments over time. A couple of new students prepaid their tuition allowing me to come up with the first and last month's rent. But signing that five-year lease challenged me. It overwhelmed me to take on such a commitment, but I had already come this far by faith. I refused to entertain that big bucket of fear the devil constantly tried to dump on me! I was confident. Not in my own ability; not at all. I just believed that what I lacked in financial backing and business education, my God would more than supply! He had opened doors for me. I was just walking through!

I hired an office administrator who wore numerous hats filling the necessary roles of maintaining student files, receptionist, and bookkeeper. She became my right hand. At last, I opened the school with great fanfare. The Grand Opening was a glorious celebration attended by many friends, well-wishers, and newly enrolled students. In the quiet recesses of my mind echoed the mocking words my children's father had said that I would never be able to support myself or get a job. The Lord vindicates His people when we give our situation to Him and do not try to defend ourselves against our enemies. He had brought me so far!!

My program was an intense four-day classroom schedule in which usually I would lecture several hours daily. I would intersperse the rigorous classroom agenda with frequent field trips, including a spectacular venture to attend Furniture Market in San Francisco. These outings were great fun for all of us. Knowing what a vital role the field trips played in our overall design school curriculum, Justin would frequently urge me to plan a trip to San Miguel de Allende in central Mexico, a preserved Spanish Colonial city loaded with historic art and architecture. He had attended art school there and knew a field trip would enrich my student's study of Spanish Colonial design, so popular in the southwest. Although I scolded him saying I had far too much on my plate to consider such a thing, he paid no attention.

A THIRD BUSINESS   One day in the early months of my business operation a vivacious lady flew in the door of my showroom making a big commotion about the beautiful pieces I showcased! She raved even more emphatically about the *positive energy* in this place! She was in a hurry to catch a plane, but before she disappeared she hastily placed her business card in my hand, saying, *"If you ever would like to offer a tour to San Miguel de Allende, Mexico contact me. I am an art historian and have been traveling there for thirty years. I am traveling to San Miguel this December and could lead a tour for you then if you like."*

With a pouf, she seemed to simply *evaporate* as she flew out the door just as suddenly as she had appeared. Justin and I burst into laughter. *"That doesn't mean I am doing a tour, Justin"*, I protested knowing full well that this was too coincidental not to take seriously.

I condescended, *"I'll put a free press release in the paper and if that sells enough to merit doing a tour I will agree to contact her to conduct one this December."*

The free press release sold eighteen tourist tickets and it kicked off the first of what became a seven-year profitable architectural tour business to Spanish Colonial Mexico! All of Tucson talked about it! David eventually took over the task of being tour director which provided a perfect excuse to get him out of a difficult situation in which he found himself in Budapest. Immersing himself in the art culture of Spanish Colonial Mexico as well as honing his budding business skills would prove to be a useful foundation for his upcoming art career. God had opened another door of opportunity, blessing, and favor.

A Journey to San Miguel de Allende
Mexico

Fleur de Lis Tours

DARREL DIES   Before opening my school Darrel developed a brain tumor and passed away suddenly. I still had the personal heartache of being separated from my two oldest children, Aria and Tim, which continued to be a constant hollow in my life. These losses kept me close to the Lord. Only He could comfort me. My God-given DNA had fashioned me to love, yet those I loved the most were now gone. I, who had never wanted a career, found myself single again, separated from my two oldest children, and deeply immersed in my career. Operating my three businesses; the school, design firm, and tour business was much bigger than I was! The person I always had considered myself to be, a loving wife and mother, was nowhere to be found. I had lost my identity! When David left for college I had no choice but to put all my energy into my work and pour my heart full of love into my students. Who was I? I would trust God to keep making something beautiful out of the broken pieces of my life.

A BROKEN RELATIONSHIP   Aria still had serious anger issues with me. I had saved her Christmas card to open Christmas morning, with great anticipation hoping for a sweet message. Instead, what I read devastated me! This message spelled out her inability to deal with me any longer. In so doing she announced that she was *"Officially severing our relationship"!* I was cut to the core. My heart was inside-out; raw and broken! Would this be my ruination?

I responded with the suggestion that we meet for a weekend at some neutral location to try to work through the issues, but she wasn't ready. Her *'truth'* didn't have any room to hear another perspective of the past events that had estranged us. The damage had been done; whether I was right or wrong I hadn't been able to break through her issues with me. By rejecting me, she was also rejecting the Jesus I served and many other values I held. The enemy hit me where I was most vulnerable! My emotions were raw! I juggled heart-ache, self-pity, and guilt alternately, eventually realizing that the message that card contained could destroy me! I would not let the devil win this battle!

My zeal for God had hurt Aria. I had reached an impasse with her. With God's grace, I entrusted my lovely girl into His able hands. In tearful brokenness, I cried out for His mercy, *"I cannot change what is past. I give her to you, dear Lord. Keep her and restore our relationship as only You can."* And I prayed for emotional healing for both of us. Slowly peace flooded my soul, not as the world gives, but I knew the heart of the Father had heard my prayer with tender compassion. I knew she would be safe in His hands. My prayer was not complete until I added, *"As my life goes forward, Lord Jesus, grant that we both might become all we can be for your glory, my dear, beloved Jesus!"* With God's grace, I surrendered Aria to the Lord to the best of my ability and I determined to move forward with His grace. It was so hard.

He works in such mysterious ways. Over the years most of my students were young ladies, many of whom became *my daughters*, if only for a season. It was a wonderful opportunity to pour wise counsel, love, and compassion into their lives that I was not able to share with my beautiful daughter in that long season of separation. Indeed God bestowed such grace upon me. His grace covered my heartache. Occasionally, especially when my workload became too heavy and I was tired, my emotions would weaken and I would weep... warm, hot tears of love for the daughter from whom I was estranged and my adventuresome son so far away from whom I seldom heard. And God was working humility into the mosaic of my life; a once-proud mother was now sorry for mistakes I had carelessly made and the hurt my children felt at my hand.

DREAM CAMPUS   Eventually a property became available to purchase which seemed to be the solution to the very dream campus I had originally envisioned when I started the school! I had become very content with my current facility so when this property became available I no longer had even been thinking about it! It seemed like my vision was being resurrected!

This historic property was an in-town former small private art school/ residence sitting on nearly four acres. The location couldn't have been more visible or ideal, on the well-trafficked main thoroughfare to the Tucson airport. It was constructed of adobe brick with brick floors and floor-to-ceiling windows supplying a great source of natural light. My designer's eye immediately began to picture how I could create a new, updated facade and revitalize the property. It seemed too good to be true. I knew just what to do to make a weary-looking structure look fresh and inviting! I would replicate what God was doing with me; making something beautiful out of something broken!

Another offer was about to be presented to the seller the next day at 2:00 PM! If I wanted to make an offer, the realtor said, it must be before the other offer could be submitted! There could be no delay!

We were still writing the contract at ten o'clock the very evening I had toured the property. There was only one problem. I still had three years remaining on my current five-year business lease. We wrote the offer contingent upon my being able to get out of my lease and it must be accepted or rejected at the time of its presentation, ahead of the other prospect!

The next day David and I were on the plane with a large tour group heading for San Miguel. At the appointed time he made a call using the phone on the seat in front of him to determine the outcome of our offer. When he announced that the offer had been accepted the entire tour group as well as others on the plane congratulated us and wished us success with rowdy whistles and applause. It was an unforgettable moment and one which set a festive tone for the entire tour!

I believed God had saved this property for me in response to the vision I originally had for my business. I claimed it as mine and something really silly became my sign that I would be able to somehow get out of the three years remaining on my lease! Dr. Sublette was the lease-holder in the large suite adjacent to my rented business space. His name was a sign to me that indeed he would sub-lease my design business rented suite!

When I asked Dr. Sublette if he might be interested in having the first option to lease my space should I move, he adamantly refused, saying, "Sad to say, Marjorie, you are one week too late! Just last week I signed a five-year lease on another thousand square feet in our business complex to expand my gallery!" Yet, how could he resist this opportunity?

Despite his refusal, he reneged, signing the new lease right on schedule. With a name like *'Sublette'*, he was surely destined to sign! And it was so!

With the contingencies settled, we moved in over the Christmas vacation. Moving all the materials, supplies, and furnishings in addition to conducting a remodel was chaotic and hectic. But it all got done and the results were perfect. My school/design-firm/tour business was spectacular! And it was all because of God. He put it all in place! Every piece of it!

ARIZONA INSTITUTE OF INTERIOR DESIGN
REMODEL/ BEFFORE

REMODEL/ AFTER

NEW FAÇADE & SIGN

SNACKROOM & MARJORIE IN SALON

CLASSROOM

One year my institute and design firm were the main feature at the Tucson Home Show. We had three days in which to erect a log cabin in the center of the arena, complete with all furnishings, appliances, custom window treatments, and floor coverings. That included borrowing a gorgeous copper bathtub from an up-scale plumbing supply house. Everyone was talking about it! Raffle tickets were sold which meant someone left the Home Show that weekend as the new owner of a log cabin!

I learned something that weekend. Next time I am tempted to say *"That sounds like a fun project!"* I need to stop and recognize what that probably means is, *"That sounds like a lot of* <u>*work!*</u>*"*

LOG CABIN–MAIN FEATURE AT THE TUCSON HOME SHOW

MY OSMOSIS   I now was the owner of an interior design post-secondary school, an interior design firm and showroom, and a cultural tour business. One of the design projects done by my firm was featured on *"This Old House"* national TV. I taught all the classes of my complete and diverse curriculum, as well as my own recruiting and placing of the graduates. Who was I? Superwoman or insane...this housewife/mother turned into a business guru?

What had happened to the old me through this mysterious osmosis? I look back on those years in awe wondering how I handled such a constantly demanding load...that frail little girl who had been bed-ridden with rheumatic fever, and was left with a heart murmur! Me, the young wife and mother whose husband almost convinced her that she would never succeed. Me, the young woman that never wanted a career. There is no answer except that God surely energized and empowered me to do the impossible by simply believing Him. He had been at work in this young lady, doing a Herculean task through a small, yielded vessel by choosing the *"foolish things of this world to put to shame the wise"* (1 Cor. 1:27 NKJV). I was making Him famous, just as I had asked.

My school was nothing short of a miracle. God had given me a vision for which He had supplied the faith to believe. It was all His. I was just the vessel through which He worked. He empowered me to do what often seemed impossible! He was writing His story through my life. Yet, sometimes I would wonder if my life was bringing glory to God. I wanted my life to count, but doubt would sometimes hound me He reassured me so tenderly:

"Your life brings glory to Me, My child because you are a spectacle to the angels!" This puzzled me, but I wasn't satisfied until... *"Because angels never sinned they have likewise never walked in faith. But they can look through the crystal sea in heaven to watch your life to see how it is done! And they marvel!"* And I smiled and was satisfied.

He was making a beautiful mosaic out of the broken pieces of my life – one piece at a time.

CHAPTER 9

MY SIFTING

ORE CHANGE   Juggling my three businesses took all my attention, but truly it was a labor of love. I loved the challenge of every design project. Interior design was my passion! Especially fulfilling was pouring into the lives of my dear students. Each new student would add another dimension to the class dynamics. The tour business brought another facet to complete the business mixture. Having David on board guiding the cultural tours, housed in an adjacent school office was just the frosting on the cake!

As enjoyable as my work was, my demanding schedule did not allow time for any personal life at all. One morning I woke up and asked myself was this the way I wanted to spend my life? Ten years into my business, with prayerful and thoughtful contemplation, I would try to sell my business.

The logical place to start marketing my design school was to go to another college to promote selling my program to its owner. So that was exactly what I did. The owner's son, interested in owning his own design school, separate and independent from his father's college, became the immediate buyer! It was meant to be!

Change came quickly! And with change came another piece in the mosaic of my life.

The buyer asked me to stay on board as director of his school; I continued to run the school as before, but new instructors were hired. My days in the classroom were over. In addition to the interior design certificate curriculum he bought from me, I wrote curriculum for other programs including bachelor degree programs in Fashion Design and Fashion Merchandising. I expanded my old interior design program into more well-rounded associate degree and bachelor degree programs that met the requirements of the accreditation board under which the school operated. The Lord in His infinite wisdom was stretching and expanding my skills to prepare me for yet another unseen chapter that would come soon enough.

Although it was agreed that classes would continue to be held on my campus, its building didn't adequately accommodate the rapidly growing student body, especially with additional programs. The new owner bought a larger facility, breaking his contract with me to lease back my campus. I suddenly found myself holding a hefty mortgage on my now vacated property. I had to think fast to find a use for that four-acre campus property that I still owned. My campus bordered an up-scale housing development whose strict restrictions challenged my options. My property's monthly payments were too high to ignore. I must come up with a solution quickly!

"Help me again, Lord. Your servant is calling!" As I called out to Him I would hear Him say,

"Trust in the Lord with all your heart and lean not on your own understanding" (Prov. 3:5).

This had been an essential life-verse to guide me in decision making. My impulsive nature had caused me to make hasty decisions in the past that I would later regret. Experience had taught me! Now as I waited on the Lord an ingenious inspiration overtook me:

CREATE A landscape design private post-secondary school!

As the Lord unfolded a solution I marveled at how He had already prepared me for this next step just as He had prepared me to operate an interior design school prior to starting my own school! Of course! My four-acre campus provided an ideal canvas for students to design and execute hands-on landscape projects! My research had revealed that there were no other private post-secondary schools in the country specifically targeting that subject! The fact that I had always been notorious for having a *'black thumb'* didn't phase me. It only reminded me of the Lord's sense of humor! I would need His direction and guidance every step of the way!

The program was stellar! Its curriculum contained a balanced potpourri of the science of gardening; botany, horticulture, and plant materials, as well as the art of design, including drawing, hands-on and computer drafting, and principles of design. The business aspect of landscape design and construction were included in the curriculum to provide the student with marketable skills. Each student had a laptop computer, in which his designs were filed, including a major real-life final project. With their design projects at their fingertips, the student could conveniently present their design projects on job interviews. To round out the program was a History of the Garden class, always a favorite! This program offered hands-on assignments with every class that could be facilitated on my campus. Instructors for each course were professionals working in their field. The school became licensed and students began coming from far and wide, about one-third of them from out of state!

MEET MILTON

Milton came into my life during this process and it seemed to be perfect timing. He so wanted to be my knight in shining armor to mend the hurts I had gone through and to fulfill my dreams. Since the loss of Darrel I had been lonely and felt that Milton would fill that void in my life. We had a small, intimate candlelight wedding ceremony in my college campus main salon, followed by a catered French dinner. We were so happy!

Another new chapter had begun!

STRAW BALE WALL   The campus was highly visible from the long north/south frontage boundary; a bit too visible! To allow for privacy I knew a tall wall enclosing a large chunk of the property would enhance the space immensely. But to build the six-foot wall I had in mind would be outrageously expensive! I doggedly considered my options and trusted the Lord to supply. His solution was so incredible I simply had to include that in this book!

A building technique that is sometimes employed in the Southwest is constructed from bales of straw. If properly constructed it can be a well-insulated, sturdy, and relatively inexpensive building material. Houses are sometimes built using this method of construction. A foundation is poured into which vertical steel rods are embedded. Upon those rods, stacks of straw bales are impaled. The entire wall is then wrapped and secured in place with chicken wire. Finally, several coats of stucco and paint complete a very handsome and durable, rustic wall.

The Lord had inspired me once again. I did my research, hired a contractor, and started advertising for my *'Straw Bale Wall Construction Classes'*. Why not let students build the wall and pay me for learning the technique! The cost of the training was quite reasonable, but after several fun-filled Saturdays my campus dream wall was in place and I even made money on the project! One of my students who owned a landscape supply business traded a large stone fountain for partial tuition payment which became the focal point of the *'back yard'*. Eventually students created a butterfly garden and a meditation garden in sections of the newly designed space.

The Lord made everything beautiful in His time, and I stood back, absolutely marveling at His handiwork! He had given me the inspiration for the school, taught me how to write curriculum, and provided my beautiful in-town campus complete now with a gorgeous wall. He provided numerous well-qualified instructors and a steady stream of wonderful students came from many states far and wide. It was all to show Him off! My part was simply to believe; *to trust in the Lord with all my heart and lean not on my own understanding.* And I was NOT a gardener! I stood simply amazed at what He had done!

MY CLASS BUILDS THE STRAW BALE WALL

DISASTER   Then came the infamous day in which a bomb dropped in my lap for which I could never have been prepared. Private post-secondary schools are required to submit an annual license renewal application. We had gone through this routine every year since our school had received its first probationary license to operate. It meant sitting in on the annual board meeting in Phoenix. This time Milton went alone as I stayed back to mind the school. We were unprepared for the catastrophe that ensued! Immediately following the meeting his phone call to me detailed the event. Stunned and in disbelief he blurted, *"We were accused of not having submitted the required license renewal application. Our license to operate has been denied!"*

I couldn't wrap my mind around that shocking announcement! *"How could that be? I have the receipt from Fed Ex verifying that we did make a timely submission. We can surely prove that!"* Other equally false or minor violations were cited. Immediately following that board meeting our local newspaper printed untrue stories reported by the board's executive director that our license had been *denied*. This resulted in the loss of two classes ready to start at a hefty loss of income. My flawless record and pristine reputation of more than twenty years in the private post-secondary school business had suddenly become history! Denying our license to operate without a hearing violated Due Process and the First Amendment as well as the board's regulations. We were just beginning to see the abusive power of a state regulatory body with little oversight. It was unbelievable!

We were told that there would be a Settlement Conference in which the executive board would be present allowing me to respond to the citations with a follow-up meeting for their decision to be heard. In reality, the Settlement Conference was a farce in which we saw absolutely no justice! The executive director refused to read the responses we had professionally prepared, at no small expense; the board was not even present, nor did they ever hear my responses to the false accusations.

The deputy director of the board told our students to contact them directly with any complaints they may have thereby bypassed our legal grievance policy, encouraging them that should our school close its doors (which they were assured would happen) the state held a fund that would reimburse their tuition. This created tremendous chaos! Milton and I lost all authority in our beloved school. Students no longer believed us when they found out that our story did not agree with that of the board. We were now *'liars'*, could not be trusted and essentially became the 'enemy' in this battle being waged against us by the board. Students wrote letters to the board claiming untrue atrocities just to hasten the closing of the school so that they could recover their tuition by the state's recovery fund. We were devastated and shocked!

Besides, the board ordered no collection of tuition or enrollment of new students to *'protect the students'*! This open-ended denial of allowing us to collect monies indefinitely from our students was another violation of a state statute and was also designed to close our doors. As long as we were in the appeal process we could continue operating, but without collecting money from students or being able to recruit new students we were surely doomed. By cutting off the school's source of income closure was illegally being enforced!. They began informing students that our doors would be shut in thirty to forty-five days.

The ensuing months became a nightmare of slanderous and untrue newspaper articles. Many of our dearest students and faculty members bitterly turned against us. There were months of daily headaches, stress, confusion, betrayal, and heartache.

PROPHECY   Several months before the school closed a student came into my office with shocking news. She had moved to Tucson from Pittsburgh to attend the institute, fulfilling a longing in her heart to become a landscape designer. She was a devout Christian with strong prophetic gifting. I respected her and we had become friends. But on this particular day, she choked back tears as she blurted out the prophetic vision she had witnessed that very morning!

"Marjorie," she gasped. *"I had a vision in which I saw an avalanche rolling down a steep mountain. As it rolled along it picked up debris, which represented the students and professors of this school. It kept rolling and gaining momentum until it came to a screeching halt hitting a brick wall! The*

avalanche is the school. You will lose the school, but God will begin to shower you with more grace than you have ever before experienced."

A devastating word. Since I had been trusting God for a good outcome her words were difficult to swallow just then. In due time it would make sense. A few days later a highly respected deacon of my church took me aside and gently gave me the very same word as confirmation.

CORRUPTION   Eventually it boiled down to a lengthy series of state hearings. Sadly, even these hearings denied due process since the administrative law *'hearing officer,'* not an official judge, could only make a recommendation rather than a ruling. Students were told by the executive director of the board that regardless of the hearing officer's recommendation the board had full intention to close the school anyway. The *'hearings'* were a farce! Coincidently, those hearings were governed by the same branch of government as our regulatory agency which explained some of the obvious bias. They were all in bed together.

The last straw surfaced when our chief witness, a former board member, was denied her rightful testimony for us. The hearing officer claimed that her testimony would suggest a conspiracy against the board. This was the one witness who could testify of the lies the executive director told the board about us. Her unexpected phone call to me one afternoon shed light on the root of the corrupt and unjust treatment I was receiving at the hand of this governing board.

All this time I couldn't imagine what was going on. My business ethics had been pristine. All those accusations were untrue. What was the underlying root of all of this? Then came a definitive phone call.

"Marjorie, as you know I have been on our state's regulatory agency for a long time. In all my history here I have never seen such corruption as you are experiencing at the hand of the board." Her call was quite a shocking expose. She continued with compassion for me and indignation toward the elected president of the board. *"I have observed your character and conduct over many years. You have had a flawless, impeccable record. That is, until recently when the president of the board began*

slandering and falsely accusing you. Because of his power and position his lies convinced the executive director, deputy director, and board members that your license to operate should be revoked!"

Wow! Now some things began to make sense. The person to whom she was referring wore three hats; he was the individual that had purchased my interior design curriculum, now my employer, also the president of the board which governed my school. He also was on a mission to put me out of business! This explained why he never recused himself as my employer from the official board meetings in which I was being challenged. Milton always contended that he was jealous of me. The landscape curriculum that I had designed should have been his idea. After all, he had grown up in the private post-secondary business. He was THE shark! If I lost my business it would position him to purchase my curriculum and pick up my in-town four-acre campus for a song, adding my landscape design program to his other design offerings. He had expressed to me many times that he wanted another design program to complete what he already offered. Now as the elected president of the board he was in an ideal position of authority to accomplish his dream.

After four grueling hearings in which the board members were never present to hear my responses to their accusations, the court official finally made her infamous conclusion to the case. She repeated herself three times to further emphasize her point: *"I'm sorry to say that I am not able to be of assistance to you. I recommend that you seek justice from the governor's office, the press, and your legislators."*

We were speechless. Could this be happening in our own democratic United States of America? Isn't this the land of freedom of speech and due process? Where was the justice? Although the hearings did not provide justice I was determined to at least try to recover some of our enormous losses. Our beautiful, historic campus property which had been my retirement security went into foreclosure. After numerous trips to the Ombudsman, the governor's office and various institutes for justice my quest eventually led me to recant my sad tale of injustice to a few attorneys. Without sufficient funds to pay their fees, it would take a miracle to find someone to take the case.

Finally, I saw a glimmer of hope when one Phoenix attorney agreed to read my well-recorded documents. His findings were my final hope of restitution, *"I have poured over your detailed records, Marjorie. What an unfortunate story!"* He sadly recanted his findings. *"Indeed the State Board clearly had many instances of violation against Due Process and the First Amendment. This would have been a million-dollar case had it not been a governmental regulatory agency subject to corruption with whom you were dealing."*

The next words he spoke would end my quest for justice, *"But, they had the liberty to do what they did in your case. As a governmental regulatory body, they are protected by the Law of IMMUNITY!"* They were immune from being held accountable to their own regulations! The case was closed! He advised me to *"get on with my life"*!

Injustice...false accusations...embarrassment...betrayal...loss...

Pain...heartache...tears...marred reputation...

Lies, lies, and more lies!

My beautiful four-acre college campus had been foreclosed. I shall never forget that black day driving out of the parking lot for the last time with a heavy heart. Everything for which I had worked so hard, the memories, the vision...it was all gone. Milton and I moved our student files and personal desks into the large media room in our home in the Tucson Mountains. Some of the finer furnishings came with us, too. The rest was sold or hastily packed and put into storage. It was over. As we silently drove home I was numb! I knew that God was with us but a door had surely shut. A difficult, stressful chapter had ended. I was weary and confused. Yet I held on to my conviction that when God shuts a door He will open another. I questioned, *"Now what, God? What door will You open now?"*

125

But, the sifting was not over. The stress placed on Milton and me throughout the entire painful process with the State Board took its toll on our marriage. I had put up the monies to start the institute and was its president and official owner. In an attempt to cover mounting expenses and rescue a sinking ship Milton frequently dipped into my life savings without consulting me until the account was drained. I didn't know anything about this until I went to the bank to make a withdrawal!

My life savings were gone...withdrawn without my knowledge...by my husband! The guilt he shouldered, his sense of inadequacy, in addition to the pressure of the failing business, brought out his old demons. Ugly anger fits and bitterness arose out of the darkness of the situation.

After several months of contemplation, depression, and rising anger over the events of the previous couple of years, Milton decided to start a new business. Although it could operate anyplace he could take a computer, he made a move to Florida for an indefinite time, insisting that a former associate there would counsel him on the start of his new business.

The day Milton called announcing he was filing for divorce I was shaken beyond belief! I wept copiously for a long, long time; deep, gut-wrenching sobs, as I surrendered to the Lord my hope of having a happy marriage. Truly, it was not just the loss of Milton; the strife of being in his gloomy, angry presence would no longer weigh on me. Rather I grieved the loss of the thing I had always desired, longed for, dreamed of...a loving marriage.

Devastated and broken, I set my will to not become bitter, but to trust my Lord and Savior with my newly shattered life. I would wait upon the Lord and He would renew my strength. He would once again put together the pieces in the mosaic of my life. During those bleak months, my faith remained strong only by the grace of God.

The months passed. I never dreamed that I would lose the school that God had given me. I had hung on so tenaciously. I had lost my business, my beautiful college property, my life savings, my children were still keeping their distance and my beautiful home in the Tucson Mountains was in foreclosure. Now my marriage was history!

SIFTED AS WHEAT   I had been sifted as wheat! In Luke 22 at the Last Supper Jesus had been speaking with the disciples about how to be great in the kingdom. They all seemed to want to hold the position of power in the kingdom, so Jesus taught that it was only by serving one another they might become great, setting an example, as usual, by serving them.

It was in this context that Jesus spoke directly to Simon Peter: *"Simon, Satan has asked permission to sift you as wheat"* (Luke 22:31). Jesus comforted Simon Peter by saying that He was praying to the Father that Simon's faith would not fail during this trial.

Although Simon Peter did deny Christ, the Lord's amazing grace toward him, as well as the shame of that event, made Simon Peter the most passionate of followers! Passionate to live the rest of his life poured out for his Master... passionate to walk the deepest walk of faith just as his Lord had prayed...passionate to the point of not feeling worthy of dying the same crucifixion as his Lord. Instead, he insisted on the more excruciating death of being crucified upside down after enduring nine months of absolute darkness and monstrous torture being manacled to a post in the vilest of prisons. Indeed, his faith not only did not fail but glorified the Lord and shone as a beacon for the world to see. That Christ allowed Satan to sift Peter as wheat indicates He had confidence that *"what the enemy meant for evil the Lord would use for good"* (Gen. 50:20 KJV). The very weakness in Peter would become his strength as that sifting accomplished its complete work. Peter would become the leader among the disciples, providing great strength to them just as Jesus had prophesied. So firm became Peter's faith that Jesus gave him the name of Cephas, meaning in the Greek translation, *a 'rock'*. Peter became the pillar of the church, preaching to the masses in Jerusalem on the day of Pentecost.

The Lord had allowed me to be *'sifted as wheat'*. The season I was losing my landscape design school gradually became a period in which I experienced great loss, betrayal, disappointment, and misunderstanding. There were times when even the Lord's presence was distant...times when the enemy's lies seemed louder than the still small voice that usually guided me...times when doubt struggled to push aside my faith.

This story of Peter reminds me that Jesus had great confidence in the ultimate victory Satan's testing would produce for the kingdom as the Lord himself would guide, embrace and lead Peter step by step through his valley. He surely did the same for me, too, as I chose to walk by faith while He allowed me to be sifted. As I reflect upon those years I now recognize that sifting was a necessary ingredient in my life for the Kingdom's sake

CHAPTER 10

HIS WORD IS LIFE!

HIS WORD ALIVE IN ME   Having suffered much loss became a desperate formula for seeking God! I found Him in His Word; His Word nourished me, gave me direction, comfort and hope! Its transforming power became the very fuel I needed to become what God designed me to be when I was in His mind at the beginning of time. There were many things I could not have done in my human weakness; my flesh. But His Word in me empowered me to accomplish the impossible. It will do that for you, too.

I could never have forgiven those that wronged me, but when I read about the consequences of unforgiveness and that God commands us to forgive, I surrendered to that Word. By forgiving those that had wronged me I could live in the freedom that only complete forgiveness provides! Sometimes I would have to repeat the process of forgiving that one that had wronged me several times. I discovered that forgiveness can be a process. Maybe that's why Jesus said to forgive seventy times seven.

My losses gave me plenty of cause for bitterness and regret; I could have justified looking back and feeling sorry for myself. But God's Word said to *"Forget the former things, do not dwell on the past!"* (Is. 43:18) and *"No one who puts a hand to the plow and looks back is fit for service in the kingdom of God"!* (Luke 9:62). I took those Words to heart and applied them to my life. I discovered that by looking back in regret I would lose my joy, but by believing His Word I would have victory and be energized with His power. I was learning a new way to Live. As I believed and applied the Word of God I became strong and empowered to move forward with hope!

I read that *"...the Word is God"* (John 1:1). Gal. 2:20 reads, *"I have been crucified with Christ. It is no longer I that live, but Christ lives in me"*. His essence dwells within me. If He is the Word and He lives in me, then the seeds of His Word are alive within me, too! As I surrendered more and more to Him by dying to my fleshly habits, sins, and desires, resurrection life would become the trade-off! I would become more sensitive to His gentle conviction resulting in desiring to be fully obedient. In so doing my mind, heart, soul, will, and attitude were being molded into His likeness.

How powerful! My broken self was being renewed and transformed through the Energy, Life, and Love of God's Word! I was not the same person as I once had been. I could weather the storm. I was becoming confident. My circumstances did not define me. As I digested the Word my faith became stronger, I was becoming who God created me to be and the Living Word became the foundation of my life!

I read and believed when He said *"'...I know the thoughts that I think toward you,' says the Lord, 'Thoughts of peace and not of evil, to give you a future and a hope. Then you will call upon me and pray to me and I will listen to you'"* (Jer. 29:11 NKJV). That Word, too, produced enormous confidence in the renewed pieces of my life! I was becoming the Word by believing and absorbing it! Isn't that simply incredible?

When I read about thinking on positive things *"... things that are true, noble, right, pure, lovely, admirable, praiseworthy"* (Phil. 4:8) I surrendered to that, as well. I surely did not want to defile that Word by partaking in unlovely thoughts. I was convicted and took that Word into my innermost being; masticated and mediated upon it until I absorbed it!

When the Lord admonished me to *"embrace every season that I am in"*, I surrendered to that Word, too. Now I approach my life differently than before. Like Paul, *"I have learned to be content whatever the circumstances"* (Phil. 4:11). It is so liberating to live in the moment. Ps. 91 tells me that *"He will save me from the deadly pestilence and that I will have a safe refuge in Him...He will rescue me and set His angels to watch over me. He promises to answer me when I call upon Him."* I believe those promises because He has been faithful to keep His Word to me so many times already. His Word never returns void. That Word, too, is alive in me.

Sometimes it has seemed impossible to conform to what the Word tells me to do. I would tell the Lord, *"What you are asking of me is just impossible! My spirit is willing, but my flesh is weak. But I have invited you to live in me, dear Jesus. I will be the vessel. Just energize me to be what your Word says. Where I am weak You be my strength!"* And so often His strength has just been waiting for my weakness to call upon Him so He could demonstrate His power. *"I can do all things through Christ who strengthens me"* (Phil. 4:13). He requires from us what we cannot do on our own! It is a wonderful thing. Why do we squirm in our own strength when surrendering to His will to work in us and go before us is so much more effective and satisfying?

I believed His promises; meditated upon them, hoped for them, declared them. Many of those promises have been fulfilled. Many promises are my reality! They have become my Life and part of my very being. What the enemy meant for evil in my life has either been restored or is about to be restored because that is what God's Word says! He is fulfilling His Word in me in such creative ways. That Word is becoming alive in ME!

Living in these uncertain times we MUST learn to not only believe the Word but meditate upon it, masticate it, digest it, live it, and allow the Word to become part of us. In Col 3:16 (KJV) we read, *"Let the word of Christ dwell richly in you, that you may live with wisdom and encourage everyone around you"*. To allow the Word to dwell richly in me is much different than to just occasionally scan the pages of my bible. It takes time, purpose, intention, and dedication.

It is a remarkable mystery to consider that He designed us to become the Word. This is a lifetime process, but very encouraging to examine one's life realizing that a Godly transformation is occurring. God is making something beautiful out of my life through the written and spoken Word! Those broken pieces of my life like shards of glass are being painstakingly reassembled to create a unique work of art for His kingdom by His Word. I am becoming His Masterpiece! It is mind-blowing! Totally amazing! He can do it for you, too!

There are plenty of things to cause us to fret and worry; to fear! But truly believing His Word is the prescription for a stress-free life; a life of power, courage, and peace! I can attest to it! *"But how does one become the Word?"* You may ask. Without minimizing Life in His Word to a mere formula here are some pointers:

1.   Hear it! *"Faith comes from hearing..."* (Rom. 10:17).
     Yes, there is a sound to the Word. Hear it spoken or read it aloud often.

2.   Declare and decree it over yourself!

3.   Believe and absorb it!

4.   Apply it!

There is incredible life-transforming power in the Word of God! *"For the Word of God is living and powerful and sharper than any two-edged sword, piercing even to the dividing asunder of soul and spirit and of the joints and marrow and is a discerner of the thoughts and intents of the heart"* (Heb. 4:12-13 KJV).

When I allow that Word to do its effective work in me it can break bad habits, convict me of sin, bring revelation, turn me around! I must constantly guard myself not to become dull of hearing or *'familiar'* with a scripture verse although I may have heard it repeatedly over many years!

As an example look what happens when one is shopping for perfume. The first spray of a fine fragrance gets your attention, your senses are quickened. But after trying several perfumes the power of each unique aroma gets lost among all the others that have been tried. The life of that fragrance has been diluted. Our senses become dull. Oh! May our spiritual senses never become insensitive to His Word. May it always spring forth like a fountain with fresh revelation and newness of Life every time we read or hear it. This may be a poor analogy but I trust that the point will be well taken.

JEHOSHAPHAT   The stories I read about the heroes of the bible encouraged and strengthened me. If God could perform His wonders for Esther, or Joseph, or Gideon or David, He could do it for me, too.

I devoured the story in II Chronicles 20 about Jehoshaphat and his people being outnumbered by several armies coming against him. This exciting tale took on new meaning and became my mantra. The odds of Jehoshaphat defeating his enemies were impossible outside of God's intervention and wisdom. Jehoshaphat in desperation cried out to his God, *"...We have no power to attack this vast army that is attacking us. We do not know what to do, but our eyes are upon you".* How this parroted m prayer, *"I do not have the answers to my overwhelming problems, but I know the One who does. My eyes are on You, my dear Lord!"* Graciously and mercifully, the Lord answered Jehoshaphat's cry. He would answer my cries to Him, too! *"Oh dear Jesus, my prayers will be answered just as profoundly if I, like Jehoshaphat, have faith in you, praise and worship You and face my enemy with courage. My story will be equally victorious! Grant me your strength, dear Lord!"*

As Jehoshaphat stood before the Lord He said to him, *"Do not be afraid or discouraged because of this vast army. For the battle is not yours, but God's. Tomorrow march down against them. They will be climbing up by the Pass of Ziz, and you will find them at the end of the gorge in the Desert of Jeruel. You will not have to fight this battle. Take up your positions;*

stand firm and see the deliverance the LORD will give you, O Judah and Jerusalem. Do not be afraid; do not be discouraged. Go out to face them tomorrow, and the LORD will be with you".

Jehoshaphat bowed with his face to the ground...in worship, praise and obedience before the LORD. He proclaimed to his people, *"Have faith in the LORD your God and you will be upheld".* As he and his people began to sing and praise, the LORD set ambushes against the armies who were invading Judah, and the enemy was defeated! When the men of Judah came to the place that overlooked the desert and looked toward the vast army, no one had escaped!!! There was more equipment, clothing, and articles of value than Jehoshaphat and his men could carry away. There was so much *plunder*, as it was called, that it took three days to collect it. The fear of God came upon all the surrounding kingdoms when they heard how the LORD had fought against the enemies of Israel. And the kingdom of Jehoshaphat was at peace for his God had given him rest on every side.

God's faithful promises strengthened me. I would be just like Jehoshaphat! God would make a way for me, too! My prayers were peppered with His promises holding God to His holy Word which never returns void. Those days were bittersweet. I was stretched and buffeted on every side. When my faith was tried and anxiety overcame me, I found solace and peace in His Word and rested again. I became weary but learned to step from faith to faith as on stepping stones. I wanted so much to be delivered from these problems, but I learned slowly and painfully to wait upon Him and amazingly He renewed my strength and gave me the grace to wait, wait and wait some more. I knew He had His best for me and I was determined to set foot on my own promised land!

POWER OF THE SPOKEN WORD   When the angel appeared to Mary he awaited her response to bring about the birth of our savior Jesus. Mary's humble spoken word, *"Let it be to me according to Your Word!"* (Luke 1:38 NKJV) began the impregnating process. When an angel appeared to Zachariah telling him that his wife, Elizabeth would have a child, his powerful words of doubt resulted in the angel causing him to be mute for the duration of her pregnancy. His inability to speak would assure that no spoken negative words of unbelief could bring harm to the unborn child.

God's <u>spoken</u> Word was what put the stars in place; the very tool He used to create the universe. When God spoke, *"Let there be Light!"* (Gen. 1:3), indeed there was light! What power dwells in His spoken Word! If by simply speaking a Word God created our world and all that is within it, what happens when we who are created in God's image speak?

Oh! The power of our words! *"The tongue has the power of life and death, and those who love it will eat its fruit"* (Prov. 18:21). Our words do much more than simply convey information, they can curse or bless. Words can stir up rage, provoke offense or violence or destroy one's spirit. Conversely, a *"gentle answer turns away wrath",* but also *"a harsh word stirs up anger"* (Prov. 15:1).

"A good man out of the good measure of his heart brings forth good, and an evil man out of the evil measure of his heart brings forth evil. For out of the abundance of the heart his mouth speaks" (Luke 6:45 NKJV).

How many have experienced deep wounds because of unkind or judgmental words spoken? Words can become tools for building us up or tearing us down. I want my words to encourage and build others up.

The words of a jealous girl from my childhood spoke untrue, hurtful words to me that affected me with discomfort well into my adulthood. She used to often torment me by telling me I was fat. Although I still wear a small size I continue to struggle with thoughts that surely were planted by those mocking, powerful words. She had a favorite nickname for me, *"Eyebrow"*! Her words declared that I had one eyebrow that grew straight across my forehead; hence my nick-name. In my mind somehow I pictured myself with a grotesque visor-like apparatus shading my eyes. *"Eyebrow"*! After quite a few years it dawned on me what a lie that was as my eyebrows were indeed rather sparse and pale. The power of words! She had other hurtful words for me, too, but the most painful ones were those that made me question my parents' and relatives' love for me. Those words foolishly spoken by a child can cause a lifetime of hurt.

It has been said that the human tongue is a beast few can master. It strains constantly to break out of its cage and if it is not tamed it will run wild and cause much grief! On the other hand, *"Kind words can be short and sweet, but their echoes are truly endless!"* (Mother Teresa).

Soothing words release *"soothing"* chemicals just as angry words release *"anxiety chemicals"*. This holds true for the speaker as well as the listener. It is common knowledge that even plants are affected by words. Plants flourish when soft, soothing words are spoken, just as harsh, loud words can cause them to wither.

Our spoken words are not only important in this life but in the life to come, as well. *"Everyone will have to give an account on the day of judgment for every empty word we have spoken. By your words you will be acquitted and by your words you will be condemned"* (Matt. 12:36). It is a sobering thought to consider that we will be judged for all our words someday.

The words we speak influence what we become. I want to guard the words that come out of my mouth that they will become tools with which to build, create and heal, rather than to cut, wound and divide. *"Let our conversations always be filled with grace, seasoned with salt, so you may know how to answer everyone"* (Col. 4:6).

I once read that our words should be "purrs" and not "hisses"!

The six most important words: *"I admit I made a mistake!"*

The five most important words: *"You did a great job!"*

The four most important words: *"What is your opinion?"*

The three most important words: *"If you please."*

The two most important words: *"Thank you!"*

The least important word: *"I".*

What power there is in the spoken Word! When we declare the Word of God over our lives and situations, God dispatches angelic assistance. Angels are assigned to listen for His Word to be decreed and declared so that they can come to our rescue when we speak it aloud! *"Angels hearken to the voice of His Word!"* (Ps.103:20 KJV). The VOICE of His Word. Did you get that? What a pity that we don't decree and declare the Word more frequently to release angelic assistance!

Even if we cannot remember a specific verse *verbatim* angels will still be dispatched when they hear the Word. I read of a lady that was assaulted by two men one evening as she was walking home after attending a church service. The men came up from behind her and dragged her to a nearby dark alley. The woman was terrified, but remembering the message she had just heard she called out *'Feathers! Feathers!'* It was all she could remember of the evening's message from Ps. 91: *"He shall cover you with His feathers, And under His wings you shall take refuge"* (Ps. 91:4 NKJV). Her assaulters swiftly fled and she was safe!

In my daily scripture reading sometimes a verse would stand out with sharp personal clarity as if it were written specifically for me. Those are called *"Rhema"* words and I feasted on them as they provided spiritual nourishment. When I began realizing the power of decreeing and declaring God's written as well as spoken Word I was discovering a key to seeing miracles! I began to see powerful results in my prayers! No wonder the enemy does his best to distract us from knowing the Word!

It has been a humbling experience to realize I could co-partner with our mighty God by speaking His Words into being. Proclamations of *"Victory"*, *"Breakthrough!"* and *"Restoration!"* became my mantras. I would decree, *"Restoration, in Jesus' name!"* over everything that the enemy had viciously stolen from me. I loved to remind the Lord that *"What the enemy meant for evil the Lord promises to make good!"* (Gen. 50:20 KJV). I believed and declared it! God would make a Divine turnaround! I would hold Him to His Word and He would restore it all! Indeed He has brought much restoration in such creative ways! How powerful to remind the Lord what He has said. His Word always comes to pass and never returns void!

Declaring these favorite scriptures over my life brought strength and many answers:

"I will repay you for the years that the swarming locust has eaten" (Joel 2:25 NKJV).

... *"His Word...would not return void!"* (Is. 55:11 NKJV).

"Ah Lord God, Thou hast made the heavens and earth with your great power and outstretched arm. Nothing is too hard for you?" (Jer. 32:17).

"All things work together for good to those who love the Lord and are called according to His purpose" (Rom. 8:28).

"'I know the thoughts I have for you', says the Lord, 'Thoughts of peace and not of evil, plans to give you a future and a hope'" (Jer. 29:11).

"No one who has left home or brothers or sisters or mother or father or children or the fields for me and the gospel will fail to receive a hundred times as much in this present age...and in the age to come "eternal life" (Mark 10:29-30).

"...Let it be done unto me according to Your Word" (Luke 1:38 KJV).

PROPHETIC WORDS SPOKEN OVER ME   Eventually I began to sense that my assignment in Florida was about to change, but I didn't have a clear understanding of what the Lord had in store for me. Over time numerous prophetic words had been spoken over me by recognized prophets. I understood that it is important to speak those words to birth them. There was so much bubbling inside of me just waiting to emerge. There was still so much more for me to experience in my life. Although I was at the age when life slows down for many, I felt like my new life was just beginning! Many things could have stopped me from dreaming big! How can I do all those things that were welling up inside of me? I still want to do the impossible for God! Sometimes I would pray, *"Lord, let me make you famous!"*

God's *written* Word brought comfort and strength to me; the *spoken* Word in prophetic utterance over my life brought concrete hope. It is written, *"Surely the Sovereign Lord will do nothing without revealing His plan to His servants the prophets!"* (Amos 3:7). I would often remind the Lord of prophetic words which had been spoken over me.

I remembered the words my former student, Karen, from Pittsburgh, had prophesied over me that *"Although I would lose my school, I would experience more of God's grace than I could imagine"*. Time proved that Word to be accurate. Truly, the pungent sting of my losses was mightily tempered by the powerful grace of God!

I was blessed to belong to the most wonderful church in Tucson that embraced the prophetic ministry. Gifts of the Holy Spirit were demonstrated frequently in our services through words of knowledge, wisdom, and prophecy. Having a personal Word spoken directly to an individual sometimes brings hope as nothing else can. That Word builds faith and becomes an anchor upon which to cling during times of testing and trials. In the spring our church hosted the ministry of Ivan and Isabel Allum, co-founders of Highland Christian Ministries in Toronto, whose prophetic ministry was widely recognized around the world. They traveled the globe visiting churches, encouraging pastors, leaders, and congregations with vision and strategy, and by speaking personal words into their destiny. How blessed I was that Ivan spoke directly over me with Words for my future; encouraging Words regarding destiny beyond my failed business. He spoke about how there would be: *"A leaving of some things and an entering of some new things and that I would begin to see who I really am come to life!"*

He said, *"Not only is it going to happen, but I am shaking it into position now. You will see things rising. It's going to be like walking on stepping stones where you can't see the other side first. Faith will be required, but you are so ready to step into this, so ready to step into the passion of the Lord. You will be a mighty tool in the hand of the Lord."*

He had additional Words about the call upon my life calling out my gifting. Those Words were powerful and stirred me to the core. They became Life to me. Suddenly the heat of the trials I had experienced was put into perspective. The Lord would see me through. I came home from the meetings with the taped Words Ivan had spoken and immediately transcribed them so I could read them, pray into them and proclaim them! I would see the Promised Land!

Although Isabel is still doing the Lord's work, Ivan has since gone home to be with the Lord. But his prophetic words over me have come to pass in God's perfect timing.

Numerous other prophetic Words have been spoken over me which I cherish. From time to time I review them, praising the Lord for His faithfulness to keep His promises to me. I continue to declare and decree those Words which He still has yet to fulfill.

"You will see justice in your life. ...justice in your family."

"You will have great influence over younger women."

"You will be writing books to glorify the Lord."

"You have suffered a great deal in your life. The Lord will restore."

"You have been pilfered! No one will rob you anymore; the Lord will fight your battles!"

"Jesus has enabled you to obey Him."

"You are a prophetic visionary. People will stand before you as you are ministering. You will minister to groups and to one and two people at a time."

"I am going to revisit all promises and dreams. There is going to be a shout of victory coming upon your life and your head. The rainbows that used to be upon your head are going to come back."

"You have many stories to tell. You have gone through a lot of things. A lot of things you have gone through have come at a high cost. There has been a lot of opposition around you. You feel like there will never be a break for you. I am coming to bring you to the rest of the climbing of the mountain."

"In the spirit I see you walking on this path. The path is not the easiest one to walk on. It is quite narrow and it goes uphill quite steeply and then also downhill just as much! Now you would think that with this picture in mind you would have a look of exhaustion on your face. But I see you walking on this path so totally relaxed and so full of joy because you know the Lord is there for you to strengthen you and to support you."

" 'My child, in the time that lies ahead of you now, you will come to experience my joy in a whole new way and in a new measure' ", says the Lord. "'You have been so faithful and have walked the road I have put you on. You have stuck it through with Me, no matter what, and served me always with all of your heart. Now, even though the road I am setting you on is bumpy and narrow and it will maybe not be the most pleasant of rides, know that I am promoting you and that I am giving you something completely new. Soon you will find that others are following you on this path with joy no matter what they might face.' "

"'I have called you to be a leader among my people, not because you are so good and capable but because of your heart for me. You have trusted me and held onto me and have faithfully carried out all that I have given you to do, my Child. So now it is time to step out onto the new road and climb the next mountain and go through more valleys together with me.

And this road you are entering will be a road of transition and soon you will enter that new land. So press on now. Let me lead you one step at a time and fill you with my strength and my joy, Child so that you can go and conquer the world for me' ", says the Lord."

"You are like a surgeon in the Kingdom. You are going to come in and carve into the hearts of people, in the deep recesses of who they are, and pull out the blockages and the things that are hidden away that nobody can see."

Those Words gave me the confidence to trust God even though there was nothing by sight to go by. Although I knew that walking by faith was the only way to please the Lord, I recognized that even my faith must be a gift from Him; His faith, not mine. I would still dare to dream my dreams...not because of anything visible, or because of my great faith, but because of the trustworthiness of God which I discovered in His Word and by how He had proved Himself to me again and again!

And I would make God famous!!!

PSALM 71 BECAME MY PRAYER:

v. 1: *"In you, O Lord, have I taken refuge; let me never be put to shame".*

v. 2: *"In Your righteousness rescue me and deliver me; turn your ear to me and save me".*

v.3: *"Be my rock of refuge, to which I can always go; Give the command to save me, for you are my rock and my fortress".*

v. 4: *"Deliver me, O my God, from the hand of the wicked, from the grasp of evil and cruel men, for you have been my hope. O Lord, my confidence since my youth..."*

v. 7: *"I have become a sign to many: You are my strong refuge".*

v. 9: *"Do not cast me away when I am old; do not forsake me when my strength is gone. My enemies speak against me. They say...'God has forsaken (her)...No one will rescue (her)' "*.

v. 12: *"Be not far from me, O God, come quickly to help me"*.

v. 14: *"As for me, I will always have hope; I will praise you more and more"*.

v. 15: *"My mouth will tell of your righteous deeds, of your saving acts all day long—-though I know not how to relate them all"*.

v. 18: *"Even when I am old and gray do not forsake me, my God, till I declare your power to the next generation, Your mighty acts to all who are to come"*.

v. 20 *"...Though you have made me see troubles, many and bitter, you will restore my life again"*.

v. 21 *"...You will increase my honor and comfort me once again"*.

The ensuing months would bring healing, new vision, and much-needed rest. All those losses behind me were just an opportunity to see God show Himself strong as He would bring about restoration! And for Him to write His-story (history) through me!

Just as He had watched over me to *"Uproot and tear down, to overthrow, destroy and bring disaster"*, He would be faithful to watch over me: *"To build and to plant"* (Jer.31:28). And when He plants there will be fruit!

CHAPTER 11

RESTORATION

ZYON'S CUSTODY HEARINGS   With the doors of the school closed, my career behind me, my home in foreclosure, and my husband gone I was certainly a candidate for a new chapter to unfold.

While I was in the process of losing my school, David was involved in an agonizing battle over custody of his young son, Zyon. The detailed records I maintained documenting my school struggle served me well as I developed skills that enabled me to assist David with his legal court cases.

During the week David was developing his budding art business in a studio he carved out for himself on my school campus in Tucson. Every weekend he would make the arduous trip to San Diego just to see Zyon, maintaining an apartment there to house his visits. Those six-hour trips cutting into his work schedule were a drop in the bucket compared to the hilarious fun father and son had together. Those days were a valuable investment David made in Zyon's young life!

Zyon's mother, however, decided to make a major move to Texas which disrupted those weekend visits. Sadly, David wasn't able to see his son so often then. Arranging for a visitation entailed costly round trip flights for him to pick up Zyon; then return him to his mother in Texas, then fly home again to Tucson. It was an emotionally exhausting period for all of us. On one of those trips back to Texas hundreds of feet above the earth flying through the heavenlies on an Easter Sunday, Zyon made a profession of faith to ask Jesus to be his Savior with his father sitting by his side. A quiet yet glorious moment! He never forgot that eternal moment and it has proven clear that something unforgettable happened up there in the skies that Easter Sunday. God's hand was most definitely on this child's life!

We prayed often for Zyon, his safety, and a better life for him. God's faithfulness would prevail as He miraculously brought full custody to David in time. In the meantime, the original court order of joint custody with the mother as the primary custodial parent was altered. It was a happy day for us when the court finally awarded primary parental custody to David, bringing much more stability to Zyon during this important formative period in his young life.

Overnight things changed in my household in Tucson. David was diligently working as a ceramic muralist spending long hours at his studio every day. We agreed that the best thing for Zyon would be for both of them to move into my rural home where I could fill that missing maternal role in his life as his grandmother and provide the loving care he needed. My home had plenty of room for all of us. It sat on nearly four beautiful desert acres with breathtaking views of the Tucson valley below. There was room for the dogs to romp and play and my front courtyard became a playground for Zyon. With Milton gone the house would have seemed empty. But the laughter of a child and the busyness of family life filled my home. It was a sanctuary of love and comfort.

WATER COMMISSIONER   Although I had just lost my business, in God's perfect timing I now was free to devote my interests to make a secure home for young Zyon. I had always felt cheated out of raising Tim since he went to live with his father still as a child of only 12. Having Zyon in my household and often in my care was redemption at work in my own life; a buying back of lost opportunities. I took my task seriously spending endless hours playing with Zyon; reading to him, encouraging his strong creative side, and becoming his teacher's assistant, reading to him, encouraging his strong creative side. I would begin telling a wildly imaginative story and halfway through insisting that he finish. We would play make-believe over many topics.

ZYON

One of his favorite games to play was *'Water Commissioner'*...a silly game we invented of which he never tired! I would be the water commissioner, speaking commands in my deep water commissioner's voice and he would be my assistant. There would be crises too numerous to list, all of which had to do with the water table, flooding, or water supply. His eyes would sparkle and he wanted to play *'The Game'* over and over. Little did I know what I was creating at the time, because as he grew older he continued to fantasize, imagine, and day-dream, a bit too much at times. We shouldn't have been surprised, however, when later he was selected to participate as a youth member of the local City Council...shades of the game *'Water Commissioner'*.

One by one Zyon's fears slowly subsided. Slowly his painful shyness gave way to self- assurance. I would tell Zyon again and again that he was destined to be a leader. Finally, he began to believe me. As time progressed indeed his leadership qualities began to surface. Zyon filled up so much of my life during those years of loss.

Zyon developed strong protective walls of distrust as a result of early childhood issues. It was difficult for him to trust anyone. Once we took a trip in which the destination was to be a surprise. Just a couple of hours away from Disneyland we announced to him where we were going! Any kid would have been thrilled to hear such a thing, but strangely, he didn't bat an eyelash. He did NOT believe that his dream of going to Disneyland could in fact come true until we were on the grounds of the park and he saw with his own eyes billboards of the famous Disney characters. Then he was the most jubilant kid on the planet. We had an unbelievably marvelous time, just the beginning of re-building Zyon's trust.

The provision for that trip was nothing short of a miracle! I had been promoting the sale of my landscape design school curriculum to the president of a Christian university. He met with me, discovering that my one-of-a-kind program was impressive and a good fit for his university. He agreed to buy my curriculum at a very handsome price, but would have to wait until funding had been secured for another business with which he was currently under contract.

The same governing body that was dealing so harshly with me at that time also governed his university. I had told him that after he bought my program I would celebrate by treating my grandson to a trip to Disneyland. Although eventually he opted not to purchase my program because of a possible conflict of interest with the board, he compensated me just for waiting for his previous deal to materialize. The sting of losing the sale of my school to him was lessened when he gave me a generous check to cover the complete costs of taking Zyon and my family to Disneyland. God never fails to surprise me with His marvelous ways. That trip was important in rebuilding Zyon's trust and for all of us to have a well-deserved stress reliever! And it came straight from the hand of God via that kind university president.

In the meantime, Aria's life was moving forward. Strong goals fueled her determination and diligence, as she eventually graduated with honors from an Ivy League university and then from a renowned medical school. These were incredible achievements especially considering the trauma she had suffered as a girl. My respect for her couldn't have been higher! God's hand was surely resting upon her. She met and married Konnor, her own Prince Charming; a mature man that became a very compatible, adoring life partner. They began to build their marriage together in a country farmhouse on a rural acreage property, an ideal setting for Aria's taste. I was reassured that God had heard my prayers to provide a compatible man for My Girl!

WHAT NEXT?   After the loss of my school, I wondered what the next step in my life would be. I sought the Lord diligently, often standing on the deck of my Tucson Mountain home, gazing at the mountains surrounding me and the city below. Emotionally I was weary, but by the grace of God, I never lost hope. God had something for me. I hadn't come this far to drown.

Logically it made sense for me to immediately pursue a job search. My finances had been drained. But the Lord had other plans. It was time to take a deep breath and accept the rest that He offered. For years my business had made great demands on me, and even more recently as my school was crashing, a deep emotional price-tag eroded my energy as well. I felt that this was the time to be quiet, wait upon the Lord, seek His face. He promised to renew my strength. My natural tendency was always to rush impulsively. I had run into a brick wall. The Lord wanted to start His restoration process with me if I would just sit still!

BIBLE SCHOOL   I enrolled in an on-line Apostolic and Prophetic course. This was just the encouragement I needed; God's anointing excavated a deeper capacity for His Word in me and I was getting direction for my life. I learned about proclaiming the Word of God and promptly began doing just that over my life. I would especially declare that all my losses would be restored, speaking the word '*RESTORATION*' often. There was power in that mantra! I could see the effect of those words in David and Zyon's lives.

WOMEN'S MINISTRY   My pastor knew my heart for God and that I had been a bible student for many years. He asked me if I would take on the leadership role of women's ministry director in our church. Throughout my Bible School training I all ready felt I had God's hand on my life for this ministry. It was as if God's own personal training had been at work my entire life for ... "*such a time as this*".

I had lived through many of the issues women face. I had dealt with women throughout my career; in the cosmetic industry years before and in more recent years, interior design. My clients and students were mostly women. My school master would be the Father's grace and faithfulness to me through my losses and disappointments.

I had no experience in women's ministry. Frankly, in those days I had never particularly enjoyed the company of groups of women, finding gossip, jealousy and cattiness sometimes dominated them. I had no idea of how to run a women's ministry. Just the same, I felt God's guiding Hand and felt assured that this was my next step. So I waited for my pastor to anoint me for my ministry. And true to form, I waited. And I waited.

Although I had promptly accepted my pastor's offer to become the women's ministry leader, I never mentioned it again to him. But I knew I couldn't move into this role without his anointing. Waiting was becoming a way of life for me, yet my impulsive nature wanted everything yesterday! I have lived my life to the tune of, *Hurry up and wait!* Yet I was beginning to rest in God's perfect timing.

One Sunday morning as I was preparing to go to church I got the bright idea that I didn't have to be ordained as the women's ministry leader to minister to someone. With that in mind, I determined that I would invite two ladies at church that morning to be my guest on a coffee date. When our pastor invited the congregation to greet someone, I promptly introduced myself to the lady sitting next to me. In response to her comment that she and her husband had just moved to Tucson from California, I immediately insisted, *"Please be my guest for a coffee date this week. You need a girlfriend!"*

My invitation evoked a reaction I couldn't have expected. To my utter surprise, she began to weep with joy! It seems she had whispered a prayer to the Lord on her way to church that morning asking Him for a girlfriend. She had been in ministry with her husband for years and as such had dealt with many needy ladies. To her prayer she had added, *"And please, may this girlfriend be mature!"*

Trish and I became instant best friends discovering that we had many things in common. Most importantly was that she had led women's ministry groups for ten years or more. She became my right hand. Our prayer life together rocked heaven and her input to me was invaluable! Her spirit-filled life and sweetness touched me deeply!

Not forgetting my determination to minister to *two* ladies that morning, I'd had my eye on another lady a few pews away. She and her husband were also first-time visitors to our church that Sunday. I swooped in on them, eager to make an introduction. I discovered that she, too, had been in church ministry for years, but later admitted that she had never had such a bold invitation upon initial meeting. Our coffee date later that week sparked another lifetime friendship. Cherry and I could have been sisters; we were two peas in a pod! She offered her lovely home as the site for our weekly women's ministry meetings. And what a gracious hostess she was!

Trish and Cherry will always be dear to me. I am blessed to have friends like these, hand-picked by the Lord. The very next Sunday, ironically, my pastor called me forward to anoint me as the women's ministry leader. It couldn't have happened until everything fell into alignment until the team was assembled by His hand. He is always a God of order.

GIRLFRIEND'S OF DESTINY (G.O.D.) MINISTRY

I told the Lord I knew there were others more gifted than me who could be a better women's ministry leader. His response was always, *"But I have called you!"* There could be no argument in that! So I entered this new phase of my life with Him guiding me. I passionately put all my heart into it and He directed every meeting, sometimes in a most unorthodox manner. I didn't follow a script but just let the Holy Spirit meet the needs at each meeting. Yes, I was scared I would fail sometimes, but then I would see how the meetings were touching lives and I would stand back and marvel!

The Lord had so lifted me above the grief of the losses I had experienced that I became the ideal person to lead our group. I wore a mantel of His peace that passes all understanding which far surpassed my own doing. The women were watching me. If I could maintain the joy of the Lord and constantly host a bright attitude after all my recent losses surely they could rise above their own sometimes daunting situations.

We had intimate weekly home meetings. Some ladies came every week, but others only showed up once in a while. We always started out singing songs of praise and worshiping the Lord. After that, there was no telling how the meeting would go although I always showed up with a message or teaching. We had a great breakthrough in prayer for one another, sometimes just for one specific need. We became real girlfriends. No gossip. No pettiness. We learned to love one another and to take off our spiritual masks. We shared one another's burdens. The love we developed for one another spilled over into our church worship services. Our whole church began to bond more closely. It was a wondrous blessing.

On a Saturday morning every two or three months we would have a larger women's meeting in the church sanctuary. Sometimes there would be a guest speaker or I would speak on a topic in which I felt the Lord's leading. There might be a panel discussion with ladies of various ages and backgrounds forming the panel and questions coming from the congregation itself.

One time after the usual meeting in the church sanctuary we had a proper tea party in the fellowship hall. Several ladies had volunteered to be hostesses. These ladies were responsible to bring their own complete table service, tea, and refreshments for their table. A competition was held to give awards for the prettiest table settings. Ladies from the congregation would find a seat at one of the tables. The women looked stunning, dressed up in tea party attire, complete with bonnets! It was great fun. Even the pastor reluctantly attended, although we practically had to push him in the door kicking and squirming, alongside all the ladies, fine china, and fussy hats. I think he was surprised at how much fun he had. The love in the room that day was so strong, the Holy Spirit showed up and it was truly the most anointed tea party ever! It was a creative way for the women to embrace their femininity.

We collectively named our group *'Girlfriends of Destiny' (G.O.D)* and our logo was a pair of girly high heels next to a rugged combat boot. This spoke of our femininity coupled with our call to being spiritual warriors.

Our Christmas women's ministry meeting was held in my lovely home in the Tucson Mountains. The women enjoyed the ambiance my adobe brick home provided with its two grand pianos, panoramic view of mountains and the valley below, Christmas decorations, hand-painted draperies, and a home full of beautiful fine furnishings and antiques collected over many years. My home was my sanctuary and I loved sharing it with my friends.

At the meeting, one of the *'regulars'*, Sigrid, a dear German woman with the spiritual gift of discerning of spirits saw a very large angel standing at my piano. She was very moved by his commanding appearance; a powerful warring angel with bright jeweled eyes and a sword in his hand. He was doing warfare over me, especially over my home. Sigrid asked me if I had considered surrendering my home to the Lord which had been in foreclosure for some time. I had adamantly prevailed in prayer that I would not lose the house. My life savings were invested in my home as well as in the school I had just lost. It was all I had left materially. God had surely given me the house, so I had battled in spiritual warfare for it, gripping it tightly never thinking God would have me give it up. Without actually realizing it sometimes our prayers can be stubborn and unyielding, even a form of manipulating God.

The instant Sigrid suggested that I should surrender the house I knew she was right. As I laid my home on His altar telling the Lord to do whatever was best for the kingdom's sake, an immediate weight was lifted. I knew then that I would lose the house in His time. His time seemed to take quite a while. My foreclosure might have been one of the longest in history. Month after month I was sent a notice that my home would be auctioned. Month after month the auction would be dismissed for one reason or another. His timing would prove to be perfect, of course!

My David had been diligently rebuilding his life after his divorce but was hoping to meet a Godly young woman to fill that longing in his heart. In conversation with him one day I spoke to him about Juju, my friend from faraway Nagaland, India.

Her letter had been among the others in my pile of mail months ago while I was still officiating over my school. Upon opening her letter I was oddly struck with an unexpected fondness for her, almost a maternal affection. As a recent college graduate Juju had been seeking a career choice. Since gardening was her passion her friends and family encouraged her to consider a career in landscape design. Hence, she found my website as one of the only places world-wide to study this discipline. She never enrolled but she and I continued to correspond.

It seemed odd to be bringing her name up in our conversation about his wanting to meet a young lady; to mention someone so far away. But he had instantly been attracted to her beauty the moment he saw her photograph, so my suggestion was just the nudge he needed. I agreed to write to make the introduction. Months passed with no response. Later we found that she had been away from her computer for months caring for her ailing auntie so missed that infamous letter of introduction. She followed the custom of her culture and stayed in a prayer house for six weeks praying and fasting about David before responding to my email. She finally agreed to write to him to see if they might develop a friendship that may lead to a future together.

JUJU   After months of correspondence David made a trip to the base of the Himalayan Mountains, with her ring in his pocket to meet Juju face to face. They spent ten glorious days together with her uncle Jay constantly at their sides as their chaperone, as is the custom in her culture. David's marriage proposal was accepted only to be followed by months of waiting for immigration papers to be submitted, considered, and processed. Their courtship was truly one of walking by faith. Juju left her former life behind including everything familiar to her to marry a man in a foreign land whom she scarcely knew because she believed the Lord had led her. And David never wavered in his pursuit of Juju; God blessed their faith and was pleased.

Eventually, the wait was over. Juju arrived with her fiance visa allowing ninety days in which to get married. The second day she was in Tucson we all piled in the car, drove the two-hour trip to Phoenix to find her wedding gown. It was a fairy tale wedding, perfect for them. The Lord was in every detail.

JUJU

WEDDING DAY

Juju moved into our household and gradually began the lengthy process of acclimating to our strange American ways. In her culture multi-generational households were common. In our case, it was just plain practical. Zyon wasn't yet ready to be separated from me as we had bonded so tightly. We shared expenses under one roof and since the house was in foreclosure we had no mortgage payment. Since Juju and David were still just getting acquainted she felt more secure with me living there in the household.

Juju's mother had died suddenly when she was only eleven, so was raised by aunties in the family compound. My daughter Aria had become distant at that same age. Although nothing would replace Aria, Juju became the daughter I had so longed for, once again displaying God's restoration and redemption. Furthermore, she brought out the best in David, restoring to him years *"That the locust had eaten"!* (Joel 2:25).

MY LOVELY SISTER, BARBARA   After the closing of the landscape design institute I got a most unexpected phone call from Barbara, my only sister. We had been estranged for numerous years, rarely seeing one another. The enemy had gotten a foothold in our relationship from childhood stemming from a jealous spirit. The jealousy, often common among siblings, was never dealt with in our family, rather it became a stronghold causing division in my family and as for me, great heartache.

Barbara and her husband had lived in Tucson for years raising their five children in a modest Foothills home. Now with the children grown but returning home frequently with their children the house was inadequate. They finally decided to do a drastic remodel, moving out of the house into a furnished apartment for a year to get the job done right. Although they had hired an architect there were many design decisions to be made. Barbara found those constant decisions overwhelming, so she asked me if I would meet her to look over the plans and give her a few suggestions. She needed my interior design training and experience. Together we made her house beautiful, the dream home she had always wanted!

The few suggestions became many suggestions requiring shopping trips to local suppliers and showrooms; putting our heads together to make her home beautiful. Barbara generously offered to pay me for the hours I spent on her home giving professional advice, but I wouldn't think of it! She was allowed to treat me to lunch, though. So we spent many hours together bonding, renewing our sisterhood, and giggling like the teen-aged girls we had once been years ago. We never discussed the years that were behind us in which there were hard feelings. It wasn't necessary. *"Forget the former things..."* (Is. 43:18). I was just glad to have my lovely sister back.

THERE IS NOTHING LIKE A SISTER (UNLESS IT'S A BROTHER!)

The deepest longing in my heart was always to have my family restored. Regardless of the business accomplishments I had achieved nothing came close to the longing for deep family bonds. The chasm between Aria, Tim, and me never ceased to hurt and hurt deeply. Holidays would go by without hearing from them, sometimes years would go by. The Thailand tsu-nami horrified me knowing Tim could have been right in the midst of it. And I didn't hear from him. I learned to go forward with my life, but always longed for those precious relationships to be restored.

I did hope. That was what kept me going. I trusted that God would RESTORE in His way. I relied on His faithfulness. This gap was bigger than I knew how to fix. The restoration of my relationships with Aria and Tim came about in miraculous ways!

TIM COMES TO TUCSON   The restoration started with Tim. He came to Tucson for an unexpected extended visit while considering a possible relocation back to the states. His wife was pregnant with Jeni; he was pondering options for building a future. I gave him a corner of my office offering to create a position for him in my business. Just about the time he arrived, however, things in my business began to disintegrate. Tim was there watching it all happen right under his nose.

Meanwhile, since David had set up his art studio at my school, Tim switched hats and became a marketing agent/motivator for his brother. They rented an apartment together and it became a time to bond, as they worked hand in hand. It was a blessing to see them complement one another, Tim's motivational qualities were just what David needed and David's talents inspired Tim. After years of separation, the brothers were bonding as never before. Restoration was taking place!

Things didn't work out for Tim to stay. The pieces just didn't fall together. In Thailand, he had started a sailing school for another organization, but it was during this visit to Tucson that he felt inspired to return to start his own similar program. It was a sad day for me when he made the decision to go back. I had hoped he and his growing family would become a closer part of my life again. But, during those months he was here our bond was deepening. While sitting at his desk in my office cubby-hole all the injustice I was experiencing was happening right under his keen nose. I sensed his compassion and sympathy for me, but it was unfortunate that he had to sit by and watch.

Our relationship was slowly being restored. Tim's deep wounds carved out by the divorce between his dad and me were beginning to be healed. I still felt his anger toward me occasionally whether real or imagined, but I could see great progress. I felt inadequate at actually demonstrating my deep love for him, feeling his outstretched arm keeping me at a distance. I knew he, too, had been badly hurt, but the main thing was he made a hefty effort to draw closer.

In the meantime, Aria's life was moving forward. Strong goals fueled her determination and diligence, as she eventually graduated with honors from an Ivy League University and then from medical school. They were incredible achievements especially considering the trauma she had suffered as a younger girl. My respect for her couldn't have been higher!

Those days were stressful as day by day the loss of my school became more obvious. But the bright light was having my wonderful Tim under my nose for a season! It was the beginning! I still felt helpless at being able to bridge the gap between Aria and me.

It would take a miracle.

CHAPTER 12

DOORS CLOSING

THAILAND WITH TIM   The restoration between Tim and me was growing. Out of the blue Tim surprised me by sending me round-trip tickets to spend a month in Thailand as a guest in his home. Hearing that my son wanted his beautiful daughter Jeni to have my influence in her life, that she needed me, were golden words to my ears.... words that brought healing as well as hot tears to my eyes! Those painful days in which I felt Tim's anger and scorn toward me were history. I couldn't have been more thrilled! God was doing something so beautiful in putting the broken pieces of my life together like a piece of mosaic art, in His way.

The month I spent in Thailand was an exceptional opportunity to get to know Jeni. Spending time with her was like turning the clock back forty years to observe the girl version of her daddy, my Tim. She was animated, those long legs of hers always in motion. She brought smiles and joy everywhere she went. Tim took the month off from his business duties, entertained me like a queen, and insisted on paying for everything! It became a marvelous new beginning of bonding. I was thrilled to see the man Tim had become, to see the successful marine business he had created, and to just enjoy his company again.

Those nightly songfests around the piano when he was just a boy had planted some serious seeds that now were bearing fruit. Who could have known back then when he insisted on singing those old sea chanteys that his love of the sea would blossom into a successful marine business one day?

TIM, THE YACHTSMAN

LIKE FATHER LIKE DAUGHTER

Finally, however, it was time to return to the states. My bags were packed, clothes neatly laid out making me ready for a quick get-away early the next morning. I slept soundly knowing Tim would wake me at the appropriate time. His wake-up call, however, was a sound of alarm! *"Oh! Mom, I am so, so sorry! My alarm didn't sound and I overslept!"* Translated, that really meant that the two-hour drive from his condo to the Bangkok airport had now just been reduced to an impossible one hour! Good thing my clothes were spread out the night before. I threw them on instantly and was out the door in a flash on Tim's heels with little Jeni and her mom skipping along right behind to catch up! We made quite a parade darting out to the parking lot where fortunately my cab driver had patiently still been waiting! With hurried goodbye kisses, Tim's apologies echoing in my ears, we drove out of sight. The Lord covered me with an unnatural peace that passed understanding. Surprisingly, I was calm as a cucumber! I knew the Lord had everything under control! As we maneuvered in and out of traffic that morning I sent up a barrage of prayers to the throne room of heaven, all the while attending to the final touches of my personal grooming, juggling lipstick and hairbrush in the bouncing taxicab.

"Now, Lord, you know I must catch this flight. You have promised to meet all my needs and I NEED to be on this flight. It is impossible to get to Bangkok in only one hour, but all things are possible with you. Do the impossible, Lord! Your Word says that you turned the clock back for Hezekiah one whole day to meet his needs and You are not a respecter of persons. I only need ONE hour. Show your favor upon me, your servant, precious Lord. Turn the clock back for me ONE hour!"

And I decreed and declared that I would be favored by the Lord and would be on my scheduled flight without delay. All the while peace flooded my spirit and I KNEW I would be on time! After all, Jesus said, *"Everything is possible for one who believes!"* (Mark 9:24). Indeed! We arrived at the Bangkok airport in only one hour allowing me time to check my bags. Once again He demonstrated His power to do the possible! Making that trip in less than one hour was a natural impossibility. God still performs miracles today as He had just demonstrated!

When I arrived at the gate the ticket agent pulled me aside as the other passengers were boarding our international flight. I had no idea why I was being singled out. After all the passengers had boarded the agent turned to me; none too soon as I had begun to wonder if I had been forgotten. He hastily ushered me down the boarding ramp and into the plane. He kindly directed me to my seat making certain I was totally comfortable.

It wasn't until we were airborne that I realized the special attention and service I had received, the spacious seats, ample legroom, and scrumptious meal were all a result of being promoted to the first-class section of this international flight! More importantly, I had been granted favor by my Great and Mighty God, just as I had asked! It was a long, tedious flight, but I basked in the comfort and luxury that Lord Himself had provided for me! Truly, "He *always causes us to triumph*"! (2 Cor. 2:14 KJV).

Returning to Tucson was a jolt of reality; a sure reminder that with my house in foreclosure we would be moving somewhere soon. But where? When? How?

The answers came slowly, but surely.

HOLDING BACK THE FORECLOSURE   A date had been scheduled to auction my home, but some things had to be put in place before we could move. Those things fell in David's lap. He and Juju had to decide where to relocate the art business. And moving Zyon out of state would require another court hearing before we would be free to pull up stakes.

My house foreclosure was breathing down my neck as a date finally had been set for the house auction. But we weren't ready to move yet! What to do? Red-hot prayers were ascending to the heavens for wisdom and strategy. Someone informed me that if I declared bankruptcy the auction would be postponed. I didn't know of anything else to do. The actual morning of the auction found me in the city offices declaring my intention to apply for bankruptcy. With the required document in hand, I practically flew the six blocks to the court-house steps where the auction was about ready to begin, high heels clicking all the way! Fortunately, all the stop-lights were working in my favor as I had only five minutes to spare by the time I reached my destination.

The auctioneer was poised to begin and the buyer was eagerly positioned with check in hand. I sprinted up those steps like a gazelle, even if a bit out of breath, placing my document in the auctioneer's hands, thus stalling the sale of my home! I never did go through with the bankruptcy, but having obtained that document bought me some necessary time to put things in order. With that ordeal behind me and knowing I would soon lose my home, we lived there comfortably by God's grace awaiting the foreclosure for quite a few additional months mortgage payment-free.

ART GALLERY   David had signed a short lease on a 2,000 square foot art gallery in the beautiful Catalina Foothills, in which I put my business skills to work once again as his gallery manager. His dazzling art was hung in the front of the gallery with several other artists represented throughout. We had a smashing Grand Opening complete with professional musicians, food, and beverage. Off to a terrific start! Clients came with their kind good wishes; some bought art at good prices. It was a wonderful celebration!

ONE OF DAVID'S STUNNING CERAMIC MURALS

Fiore Fine Art

After April, however, the doors didn't open so often. The seasonal snow-birds had gone home. The parking lot was empty. None of the other galleries in the complex were doing business either. The well had run dry.

When David signed the lease he was given a nine-month option to see how his business would develop before agreeing to the usual five-year commitment. This turned out to be a loophole clause giving David a way out. After the nine-month trial period, just before signing the longer lease, someone came into the gallery leaving a pamphlet on the desk which promoted a gallery for rent in Santa Fe. This stirred David and Juju to consider their options seriously. Maybe Tucson was not the market for a long-term business.

A trip to Santa Fe ruled out that choice, but other options began to surface. Eventually, the decision was made. Florida seemed to be the perfect solution. The demographics were right. The population was more dense than Arizona, there was more affluence and the climate was appropriate for David's art, ceramic murals for indoors and out! David began to clean out and vacate his working studio

There was no question about it! I would tag along.

It was all about Zyon. He and I had bonded tightly. Having already been separated from his mom, I felt that another separation, this time from me, would be too traumatic for him. Although I was deeply entrenched in my life in Tucson I didn't hesitate making my decision. Women's ministry was the biggest consideration. Yet some changes were occurring in my church and I felt in my spirit that perhaps my purpose there had played out. Of course, the relationships I had in Tucson with my sister and her family and my many friends were important, but the trauma of all the losses I had recently experienced made the thought of a new start appealing.

PREPARING FOR FLORIDA   The large deck on the back of my house became the site for my colossal designer's garage sale. We were moving too far to take all my belongings. I had to pare down to the bare minimum. The sale took weeks. There was no room for sentimentality. *"Just grit your teeth, Marjorie"*, I told myself. *"Pack up your things for the sale. You are moving on!"* The Lord had given me His word, *"Do not remember the former things, nor consider the things of old"* (Is. 43:18 NKJV).

No looking back. I could only take what would fit into a 26' moving truck, and a big part of the load would be David's kilns and art studio supplies as well as the personal items of his own family. My lifetime collection of fine furniture, art pieces, books, and plants had to go. When I would be tempted to be sentimental about losing my treasures I would be reassured that it was all a part of the process of starting over. The Lord had always supplied. This time it would be no different.

It was amazing how every item was purchased by a person who was handpicked for that particular object. Everyone had a story to tell of how that specific item would be treasured in their own collection. I was especially blessed by the University of Arizona professor who came to purchase my antique kitchen pot rack, a transformed handmade iron chandelier. When I learned that he was the Arizona authority on the SW desert tortoise I immediately knew he must meet "Snappy"!

A very large desert tortoise had found his way onto our property some months earlier. We adopted him promptly dubbing him 'Snappy'! It was a weird name for a desert tortoise, but we didn't know any better. I guess we thought all tortoises were snappers! When Juju brought his pie tin of green vegetables and fruits out to feed him each morning he would hastily march out of his hiding place and follow her around, nudging his adorable bobbing head and gently nipping at her bare feet. Of course, I had been concerned about what to do with him when we moved.

Snappy was deeply entrenched in his winter nap in my courtyard when I ushered the professor to my courtyard for the introduction. They were a perfect fit! They went home that day a very happy man with his antique pot rack and a friendly fine desert tortoise, Snappy, in tow. It was a sign to me of how much the Lord was taking care of the most minute details of our move. Who would have been a better match for old Snappy?

It became obvious that it would be impossible to make the move with my three dogs, the two gorgeous Whippets, and my dear old Sebastian, a beastly, lovable Rottweiler whose size would intimidate most any intruder! Who would rent to a family with three dogs, particularly one as large and intimidating as he? Big, adorable, teddy-bear Sebastian had to go!

Sebastian was hopelessly devoted to me. Everyone commented on it. He never let me out of his sight. I had spoiled him rotten! He ate better than many people with his boiled chicken and brown rice meals twice a day. OK. I shamefully admit I let him sleep on top of my down comforter at the foot of my bed. Even if I did give him up, who would love him and spoil him as I had?

As we prepared for the move the question of what to do with Sebastian was always in the back of my mind. As the days loomed closer to moving day, this became more and more of an issue. Then my friend, Trish, called telling me her friends might be interested. So we scheduled a meeting; *The Prospective Family Meets Sebastian*. It was like a pre-arranged marriage introduction.

OUR BELOVED SEBASTIAN

The family arrived and I called for Sebastian to come and meet them! It was instant love at first sight all the way around. They offered him gourmet dog treats, which he accepted with gratitude and affection. After a surprisingly successful introduction the day arrived when they returned to pick Sebastian up for the ride to their country home...the day I dreaded!

Knowing that he would sense he was leaving I expected he would be hanging his gorgeous big old Rottie head and whine. On the contrary! He followed his new owners into their awaiting truck with a sprightly spring in his step, never looking back. My last glimpse of him was that of a very happy fella, head out the window, nose sniffing the air, ears flapping in the breeze, and tongue drooling with delight! Later I learned that in his new home he had made fast friends with two cats, was enjoying an even better diet than before, had two boys to romp and play with, and acres of Arizona countryside at his disposal to enjoy. Tragically, the family had been grieving the loss of two of their sons. Sebastian brought new sunshine into their lives as his cheerful demeanor brightened their sadness! They all needed one another and once again my problem had been solved at the hand of my wonderful Lord.

If the Lord could solve the dilemma of where to place old Snappy, the desert tortoise, and Sebastian, my big devoted Rottweiler, how much more would He take care of us in this major move? This was such an obvious tender act of love the Lord demonstrated to our family. Our faith was encouraged and strengthened.

BIRTHDAY TRIP BRINGS CHANGES   A few weeks before our move as I flew through our house about to attend a church conference David and Juju stopped me in my tracks with an excited announcement: *"Mom, we have an unexpected vacation coming up! Dad's birthday is coming up and his wife just sent us round-trip tickets to fly to Florida for a surprise celebration with him! Can you believe it?"* Tim and Aria had also received the same invitations for themselves and their families. It would be the first time they had all congregated in many years. David and Tim had been out of touch with their father so this all came as a monumental surprise!

My reaction to the *invitation* even surprised me! My initial response was shock, followed by a flood of deep disappointment that I wouldn't be part of it all. I was rattled! What a strange response! Of course, I wouldn't have been invited. Years of pent-up emotions welled up within me as I relived the hurt once again of all the things I had missed with my children. Now Tim and his family would be here in the States all the way from Thailand and I would miss them. The pain I felt because of the wounded relationship between Aria and me brought salty tears to the surface. My heart was squeezed!

Driving to the women's conference the floodgate burst open! My emotions let loose! Yet I had scarcely gotten into my good cry when I got hold of myself recognizing that my thoughts were all about my pain. The announcement about the Big Birthday celebration that my family would have together had rocked me thoroughly! What was I thinking when disappointment overcame me? My children had not seen one another in years. This would be an ideal occasion for them to bond and renew strong relationships with one another. Perhaps this could be a giant step in healing the deep wounds in our family! And so, I humbled myself, pushed myself out of the way, and asked God's forgiveness for my self-centeredness.

I now had a new resolve to declare *'increased restoration'* over my family once again! God worked all the details together for good! Oh! His ways are so far above my own understanding.... .so much better! And <u>Restoration</u> was exactly what He had in mind!

To my delight, Tim and his family decided to come to Arizona to stay with me for several weeks after the Big Birthday Party! Jeni had her school vacation. Not only did they come for a visit, but Tim was a huge help getting us ready for the move across the country. I can't imagine how we could have done without him. He took charge of the garage sale, helped with the packing, and became very involved with the whole process.

Yet I was not prepared for the report that came back to me following their trip to Florida. What they had to say was startling! Their father was cold, unemotional, grouchy, and negative. Worst of all he told them that, *"It wasn't my idea for you to come!"*

The pain of this shocking comment and his coldness would have been more unbearable if the three siblings didn't have one another. I could just picture them sitting up nights discussing the situation, reflecting on the years gone by and how unreasonable and unkind their father had been. As it turned out the Big Birthday Party became a huge turning point in the process of bringing restoration to my family; their relationships with one another as well as much deeper bonding between them and me! I was becoming the adored Mother, now somewhat unfamiliar territory to me, but I was overcome with gratitude! Miraculously, the Lord in His perfect timing was restoring years of heartache. Tim took me shopping for a new state-of-the-art laptop computer, spending the next few days giving me instruction on how to use it. He outdid himself demonstrating his kindness and love to me, thus restoring many years of hurt and misunderstanding! Something beautiful was growing in our relationship. RESTORATION!

Under the conditions of David's divorce decree, he was legally obligated to get permission from the court to move Zyon out of state. We had decided to make the move during winter break so Zyon would not miss any school. There was not a second to waste! It seemed to take longer than usual for the court to schedule the required hearing. We had no choice but to move forward with plans for the move trusting God that the court would approve the move.

COURT HEARING   Preparations had been made. With the colossal moving sale over, David canceled his lease on his working studio and cleared out his materials. Finally, with only a few days remaining before our scheduled cross-country trip, the court set the date for his hearing. Now that we were about ready to leave, with belongings sold or packed, we could only pray that the judge would comply with David's request. Imagine our elation at the judge's unexpected ruling! Not only was the move granted, but she awarded David full custody of his son! Praise the Lord! It was a huge breakthrough and really put things in alignment for our move.

Although she never came, the judge agreed to allow Zyon's mom to have supervised visits. The change of custody was completely unexpected. David had not even requested it, doubting that the courts would consider it! I believe it was God's favor for Zyon and our entire family. Hopefully, his mother would see it as a wake-up call and deal with her issues. We had compassion for her, prayed for her, and wished her the best. We prayed that in time Zyon would have a healthy relationship with his mom.

This took a great load off David's shoulders and the timing was ideal. It was the perfect blessing to start this new chapter in our lives! We were given a blessed send-off by our church with prayers and prophetic words all over us. We had high expectations regarding our unfulfilled destinies, putting our future in God's hands.

WE'VE COME THIS FAR BY FAITH   So on the appointed day after an exhausting period of packing, making preparations, and saying our farewells we slowly inched down the steep driveway with David at the helm of the 26' rental truck, towing my Audi A4. Zyon and I tagged along behind as I drove David's monstrous utility van loaded to the hilt with his art paraphernalia and my two Whippets, bedded down for a five- day haul across the country! I didn't see much of the country those five days because my eyes were fixed on the highway and the load ahead of me. As we progressed from state to state I rejoiced, loudly singing and proclaiming, *"We've Come This Far By Faith!"* I love the line in that song, *"He's never failed us yet!"*

We weren't the best prospective renters. Finding someone who would rent to us became a greater challenge than we expected. With the loss of my business, I also lost my once pristine credit rating. We were not exactly what a landlord would consider to be the ideal tenants with my recent home and business property foreclosures, David not having established credit, our being from out of state, and possessing two frisky dogs! But, finally at zero-hour with only a few days remaining till we were scheduled to leave someone decided to risk renting to us; not a moment too soon! We gladly rented the home sight unseen believing that the Lord had faithfully guided us once again.

Once we crossed the state line into Florida the tension rose within us! As we inched our way across the country curiosity had gripped us as we wondered what we had just leased. Entering our new gated community we beheld a neighborhood exceeding our expectations with beautiful Florida landscaping, man-made lakes, fountains, paved streets, and manicured lawns. The house itself was just the right size, offering a modern kitchen and laundry room, five bedrooms, four bathrooms, and areas upstairs providing privacy for each one of us. David could set up his studio in the garage. It was perfect! We were finally here! We gave thanks to the Lord for His favor and watchful eye over us as we had safely trekked across the country.

We would often reflect upon the past weeks and months marveling at God's guidance and faithfulness to attend to even the smallest details. We could only stand in awe! The Lord had brought everything into perfect alignment; making all the arrangements in an orderly fashion! He delayed the foreclosure, found all the right buyers for my stuff, arranged for no house-payments for months and provided a generous court decision for a secure future for Zyon. Everything had been done *decently and in order!* He had taken care of every minute detail! God's hand has surely been upon us neatly shutting every door behind us. Now He was about to open some new ones!

After months of preparation and waiting on the Lord our new life in Florida had begun. What did He have in store for us?

CHAPTER 13

FLORIDA HERE WE COME!

DARLING BABY BOY   A few months after our move Juju gave birth to baby Timmy, the most darling baby boy! Our household revolved around his schedule and the activity that a baby creates in a family. He brought so much joy and laughter into our home. As Juju learned to hone her mothering skills I also was learning to allow her to discover motherhood without my meddling. I had to learn to give encouragement rather than advise. I didn't always encourage enough. Although Juju was becoming a wonderful mother, her mothering style was different than mine had been. I learned that my ways were certainly not the only way. I found myself shamefully taking my ugly old pride to the cross where I chose to leave it forever. The Lord faithfully took my pride upon Himself, exchanging it for forgiveness and the immeasurable sweetness of His presence.

YOUNG TIMMY

PIANO   In Tucson I had two six foot grand pianos in my living room. One of them had been in the salon of my school, but when the school closed it found itself straddling along side of my other piano. I planned to sell both pianos before moving, but my piano craftsman/tuner begged me not to sell my antique Baldwin. *"They just don't make them like that anymore! This is a true gem! It will be hard to sell at it's true worth!"* This probably was not the wisest counsel because after the move the piano sounded terrible! The move adversely affected the piano's action, which would have been far too costly for me to have repaired. And now, because it sounded so bad it would be almost impossible to sell. This was so discouraging to me! I am a trained classical pianist accustomed to playing a quality instrument.

One day I confided my discouragement to my son, *"Oh, David, it always has been so refreshing for me to sit down and play my piano. You know how happy it always makes me to play. But my poor, beautiful antique piano just couldn't take the move. Some of the keys don't even play now and the action is really messed up! I am really discouraged. I should never have moved it!"* As soon as I poured out my chorus of complaints I regretted that I had done so. I realized too late that David wasn't used to hearing me complain like that. He took my comments seriously. A couple of weeks later our conversation would reveal exactly how seriously he had taken them.

That conversation occurred in the landing at the top of our stairs. I can picture the scene vividly. David had waited for just the right moment, *"Mom, I want to tell you something. Your kids and I have pooled our resources."* Where could he be going with that? *"We want you to find the piano of your dreams, hopefully on Craigslist; so we can buy it for you!"*

Of course, I was overwhelmed! *"Are you serious?"* Was I hearing correctly? I could scarcely take it in. Indeed those complaints I voiced to David had seriously impacted him! But there was more. *"One more thing"*, he added. *"Whenever you sit down to play just know how very much your kids love you!"* That was too much! Not able to restrain my emotions any longer, I began to weep copiously. My tears must have been contagious, because David started weeping right along with me.

That one very generous act of kind generosity from my beloved children restored many years of heart-ache!

We drove together to Miami with great expectation to look at the piano. It had been owned by a concert pianist from Austria. But when we arrived at his home there was all ready a prospective buyer in the other room playing Chopin's *Fantasy Impromptu* flawlessly. I told David, *"We may as well leave. She is crazy about that piano!"* Waiting next in line, however, was a music teacher. While I was eventually taking my turn at the keyboard she and her husband were on the porch negotiating a deal with the owner. Meanwhile the first lady had gone to check out another piano for sale although she agreed she would be back promptly to buy this one. Her father who was buying the instrument for her insisted that she look at more than one before making a final decision. David's words were prophetic, *"The last one here will buy the piano!"*

I got my turn and indeed I was the last one! The piano was stellar! It suited me to a tee. My pianistic style and technique instantly was enhanced dramatically! David topped the previous offer making me the new owner of a gorgeous six foot ebony Kawai piano! Before we left I asked the owner to play for me. He had only gotten a few measures into his piece when I recognized it to be a piano arrangement of the luscious Rachmoninoff, *'Vocalise' !* I squealed with delight. I had played this as an accompaniment many years prior for a professional singer; a vocal piece with a gorgeous haunting melody written to be sung with only one syllable, *"La"*! I had never forgotten that intoxicating melodic tone poem.

Not only did the Lord *'restore'* a piano to me, but blessed me with such a healing demonstration of love from my kids. As an added bonus the sheet music of that luscious *'Vocalise'* arrived in my mail box a few days later. David had been so touched by my joy at hearing it that he bought me a copy of the music. Although I have played it many times since, it never fails to trigger my heart-felt appreciation of that tender demonstration of my children's love for me and David's thoughtfulness at ordering *'Vocalise'*!

CALL TO PARTNER   I began looking for a church to attend. When our gated community posted an invitation for an Easter brunch at the community center I decided to attend. This would be a good way to meet some of my neighbors as well as to celebrate Easter in the start-up church temporarily being housed in our club house. A few minutes into the vibrant service I knew that I was *'home'!* The fellowship was so sweet and the presence of the Lord was powerful! As I recognized the strong anointing and gifting on the pastor, I instantly became aware that this would be my church home!

There had been so many steps leading me there that Easter Sunday. Steps that required the closing of some *"doors that no man could open"* (Rev. 3:7); closed doors that had cost me the loss of my business, closed doors that cost me the foreclosure of my home and a closed door even on my marriage

Doors would also open that *"no man could close"* (Rev. 3:7). The close relationship that developed between me and Pastor Ken Hughee and his wife, Sharon, were the beginning of doors opening. I would become a leader in that fellowship, especially in the area of intercession. More significantly, the Lord had given Pastor Ken a very unique vision which he felt led to share with me. When he shared it my heart skipped a beat! I would buy into that vision, too! What seemed like his impossible dream became my dream, too! It was a dream that only God could accomplish. God had done the impossible in my own life and I knew from experience that there is nothing too hard for Him. I would partner in faith with Pastor Ken, support and encourage him in his challenging vision. I knew that with such an immense vision Ken would be target of the enemy's snares and evils.

I would *'stand in the gap'* for him.

Ezekiel 22:30 speaks of *'standing in the gap'*! *"I looked for someone among them who would build up the wall and* <u>*stand before me in the gap*</u> *on behalf of the wall so I would not have to destroy it, but I found no one!"* Israel's walls were in disrepair making the city vulnerable to enemy attack! With broken spaces in the wall the Lord was looking for watchmen to stand in those *'gaps'* to protect the city's inhabitants while the wall was being rebuilt.

Watchmen were vulnerable to attack by standing on the front lines. They were the first ones to take a hit when the enemy approached instead of those they were called to protect. But He could not find anyone willing to take the risk. Perhaps the risk that the position required was too intimidating! As a watchman today we must know how to be vigilant, keep a watchful eye out for possible threats and know how to guard our post with our God-given authority! *"Never be silent day or night to call upon the Lord..."* (Is. 62:6), going without rest until our work is done. Standing in the gap is nothing to take lightly!

The time finally came when the Lord led Pastor Ken and Sharon to move to New York, positioning themselves to be in alignment for that vision they were believing God to bring to pass. They followed the Lord's leading by taking a quantum leap of faith toward that vision, which I continued to share. They sold their home, held the last service at the church and headed to a destiny they could only see through the eyes of faith. *"Faith is the substance of things hoped for and the evidence of things not yet seen"* (Heb. 11:1).

VANGUARD TEAM   After Ken and Sharon left for New York I was led to attend another church in our community. After one Sunday service the pastor prophesied that the Lord had told him I was a *'Vanguard'* team member. I hadn't heard that term before, nor had he. I was stirred with wonder and anticipation, promptly googling it when I got home: *"A Vanguard team is a person or group of people who are the leaders of a movement; at the forefront of an action or movement; avante garde, cutting edge".* That was me! I knew I had been Pastor Ken's chief prayer support and partner, but now he was in New York. This word was confirmation that I would continue as his Vanguard team member even though we would be in separate states.

BECOMING RESTLESS   There were other clues that my assignment was changing. Restlessness was stirring within me. Often a sign that change is about to occur is that God's grace begins to wear thin in one's assignment. I was in transition. With the closing of the church I felt like my assignment in Florida had come to a halt, too. I continued in prayer for Pastor Ken's vision to be realized wondering if that would mean a move for me, too?

In our household I had always shared my business skills with David as he was launching his changing art business. I used my designer's eye to encourage his color palette, built his data base, helped him write his business plan and constantly clipped magazine pictures of art for his growing and changing *idea file*. I took upon myself the cleaning of a messy art studio upon just to try to keep things in order. Slowly Juju began to step up to the plate to fill in some of those areas. As she did so, I silently bowed out, believing that it was more her place than mine even if I had training and experience she lacked. It was wonderful to see David and Juju growing together as partners and for Juju to develop her role as her husband's help mate. They were a good team! God would have another assignment for me.

Juju and I had bonded. I loved her as my own daughter! We had moved heaven with our prayers. She had bravely left her country for a new culture, knowing that I would be there to guide her as necessary. Surely she had watched me and learned from me. But, thankfully she had a mind and plenty of dreams of her own. I was so proud of the way Juju had faced her challenges, but as she became more secure I somehow felt that my assignment as her guide was fading.

Although I paid my share of the rent in our home, I felt that my role was now more of a guest in David and Juju's home. This was time for them to build their life together and I wanted them to feel that this was their home, not so much mine. My home had always been my special sanctuary, my domain, the place where I loved putting my design and homemaking skills to work. Now that I was unencumbered by my things as well as my place in the household, some of my former identity was lost. I was learning to let go.

I made the move to Florida because Zyon needed me. But now as a budding teenager, he had become more secure, he was becoming a leader and was no longer so dependent on me. I gratefully watched as the fruit of my labor with him blossomed. The season of my usefulness in Zyon's development was slowing down.

POWER OF WORDS   When Zyon moved into my home in Tucson he was a very bashful little boy. He had some emotional scars from his parent's divorce expressing itself in timidity and extreme shyness. When he went to school he would walk down the halls with his eyes looking at the floor just to avoid eye contact with other children. His shyness must have been very painful for him.

Knowing that there is great power in our spoken words I began speaking leadership into him. Every day I told Zyon that he was a leader. He would grin a sheepish little-boy grin but just didn't take me seriously. I would tuck him into bed at night declaring, *"You are a leader. Others look up to you, Zyon!"* The power those words had in his life was transforming him.

By the time Zyon was in high school, he had overcome much of his shyness. His classmates looked up to him. He was chosen to represent his school on the Youth Council, a teen-aged branch of our local City Council whose meetings were always televised. What an incredible joy it was to see Zyon on our TV screen looking so professional in his business attire and hear his confident comments. That seemingly simple game of *'Water Commissioner'* he and I had played so often those earlier days in Tucson were surely the seeds for his City Council position. God had brought him so far.

With his confidence rising Zyon applied for a weeklong leadership program at Morehouse College in Atlanta for select young high school boys the summer he was approaching his junior year. We were ecstatic that he was one of only seventeen boys across the nation to be selected! In a phone conversation I had with one of the administrators of the program I was told that Zyon related with pride the story of his grandmother's words declaring leadership over him as a young boy.

The following year he was honored to be selected to represent his school at Boy's State in Florida. I believe these achievements were the result of spoken words of leadership released into the atmosphere to make a difference in an insecure little boy's life. If those words I spoke over Zyon could have such a life-altering effect consider what else might be shaped and influenced by simply speaking words into being!

Other spoken words were having a powerful effect on my family, too! When I began to decree and declare *"Restoration in my family, in Jesus' name"* as my mantra I began to see Aria and Tim come back into a stronger relationship with me.

CHANGE COMING   Eventually I began to sense that my assignment in Florida was about to change, but I didn't have a clear understanding of what the Lord had in store for me. Curious energy was bubbling inside of me but I didn't have direction as to where it was taking me. There was still so much more for me to experience in my life. Although I was at the age when life slows down for many, I felt like my new life was just beginning! Many things could have stopped me from dreaming big! How can I do all those things that were welling up inside of me? I still want to do the impossible for God! Sometimes I would pray, *"Lord, let me make you famous!"*

As I considered that *"The Sovereign Lord does nothing without revealing His plans to His servants the prophets"* (Amos 3:7), I decreed words that reliable prophets had spoken over me. In addition to earlier prophesies I had received some more recent words were: *"Everything NEW!"* *"Prosperity"*, *"Encouraging others"*, *"Deborah anointing"*, *"Strong as a lion!"*, *"Barnabus spirit of encouragement"*, *"Dreams revisited"*, *"Abundance, overflow and fruitfulness"*, *"Vanguard team!"*, *"Very big doors will open soon!"*, *"Writing books!"*

BABY EAGLET   Despite all those powerful words I was still tempted to be discouraged at times, especially when I looked at my situation rather than put my total trust in God. I was that baby eaglet whose wise mother had begun to pluck the comfortable, cushiony feathers from the nest to motivate her chick to discover the bigger world beyond. The sharp twigs and sticks began to probe and disturb! I was being pushed out of the nest, but where was I to go?

CHAPTER 14

A DOOR OPENS

SPIRIT OF HEAVINESS

At one point I realized that I was beginning to carry around a burdensome heavy spirit. It sort of crept up on me without my realizing I had invited an unwanted guest into the sanctuary of my spirit. When the Lord opened my eyes to this sin, I was horrified and became determined to apply the anecdote His Word prescribes for such a malady: *"Put on the garment of praise for the Spirit of Heaviness"* (Is. 61:3 NKJV). I determined to always praise God and trade my negativity for praise and gratitude. What a difference it made! Truly, attitude is everything! Things that had offended me now became a target for my praise and thankfulness. Self-pity gave way to the renewed joy of the Lord, which became my strength just as Nehemiah of the Old Testament, had said: *"The joy of the Lord is my strength"* (Neh. 8:10). I could be filled with His joy any time I felt like it just by donning my regal robe of praise! It did not require my situation to change at all. Had I written the script for my ideal life my current situation was not what I would have written, but that didn't matter! I could be filled with the joy of the Lord whenever I pressed in to praise Him!!!

The Lord kindly offered me a word that became an effective tool of empowerment for a positive life. He whispered in my spirit to *"Embrace every season you are in, My Child, even if it is not your natural preference".* I needed to hear that word! It has given me freedom and satisfaction ever since that day! Learning to embrace rather than just tolerate every season and situation has given me a life of joy, liberty, and satisfaction. What a valuable word of encouragement that was... a key to a life of contentment!

With a new lightness in my step and freedom in my spirit, I decided that while I was waiting for the Lord to open doors for me I would just open a few for myself!

BOOK OF DREAMS

I remembered the prophetic word spoken over me a few years earlier that my *'dreams would be revisited!'* As a visual aid to promote the fulfillment of that "word", I put action to my prayers and that word and created my very own, one-of-a-kind *"Book of Dreams"*. This was just what I needed to boost my faith! Using a beautiful journal I all ready had on my bookshelf I began cutting and pasting words, captions and illustrations from books and magazines to creatively assemble my book. I found many quotes from T. D. Jakes book, *"Woman, Thou Art Loosed!"* which I cut and pasted. In fact, I used his title page as my first page, as I felt it was totally appropriate! I was about to be launched, or "loosed"! I dug deep to illustrate the things that mattered most to me. The journal that I used had printed quotes and water color illustrations all ready, so it formed a lovely backdrop for all my dreams.

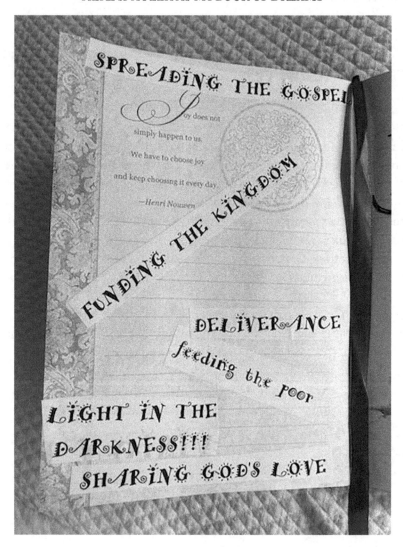

Sometimes in my prayer time with the Lord, I would hold up my book to remind Him of the dreams He had deposited in my spirit. I would declare, *"Dreams Re-Visited"*! My *"Book of Dreams"* became a prayer tool. The quotes and scripture verses it contained became my mantras.

"No good thing will He withhold from those whose walk is blameless" (Ps. 84:11).

"Seek first His kingdom and His righteousness and all these things will be given to you as well" (Matt. 6:33 NKJV).

They illustrated the desires of my heart that His Word promised to fulfill. The preface to my book contains the following declaration:

"In the name of Jesus, by the authority of God's Word, from this moment forward I do not look at myself in the natural, but according to the Word of God. I see myself the way God sees me. I am highly favored by the Lord. I am crowned with glory and honor. I take authority over condemnation, over guilt, over shame, over inferiority. That's not of God. I break its power over me. My self-esteem shall rise and be accordinnng to God's Word. I will not be high-minded but choose to walk in humility. I know who I am in Christ and I fully expect the treatment that is afforded those who are highly favored!"

There was more to my daily declaration, but I finished with:

"Doors will open for me that men say are impossible to open. Today I expect the favor of God to go before me. In Jesus Name, I am honored by my Father. I am special to Him. I am the object of His affection. And if God be for me, who can be against me? Nothing shall separate me from His love."

I encourage my readers to create their very own *book of dreams* to build faith and to become a tool of empowerment!

VOLUNTEER   I wanted to become all I could be for the Lord. As I waited on Him to open doors of opportunity I suddenly had a brainstorm: *"While I am waiting for God to open doors for me to be fruitful, I could become a volunteer in my community to be helpful to someone in need. I will become a volunteer!"*

This inspiration led me to google *"volunteer positions"*; I pulled up many opportunities, some of which I pursued without results. But one opportunity made me ask myself, *"Why not?"* This was a curious ad looking for someone to volunteer being an assistant in a cooking class for the blind and visually impaired. What a concept! I called the number in the ad and scheduled a meeting for the next day to get acquainted with the director before the class.

That was when I met JANICE! That meeting was without a doubt a Divine appointment! As she and I exchanged stories while sipping iced tea in a local cafe it seemed that we were both gifted with big faith; ready to embark on a purposeful "rest of our lives"! Janice and I had so much in common. Not only did we share similar talents and gifts but we both DREAMED BIG! There was an immediate bond.

Janice had nearly lost her vision as a young woman, many years earlier, plunging her into the world faced by blind people; an often hopeless world of darkness. Having lived as a blind person in our culture she understood the difficulties many sightless people face; helplessness, inadequacy, isolation, and loss of self-esteem. She developed an organization to bring greater respect and dignity to the blind, infusing its members with hope and inspiration to live more satisfying lives. Her organization hosted gourmet cooking classes, golf lessons, fishing expeditions, and dance and fitness classes! There were so many people to be helped; a staggering figure of 70,000 blind people in Palm Beach County alone!

Janice had been praying fervently for a mature woman to be her assistant; a Christian woman with an entrepreneurial background, a visionary, a confidante. I fit the bill. Was I to move ahead by adding Janice to my Vanguard team, too?

I spent the next afternoon assisting in the cooking class taught by a professional chef with quality food generously supplied by a gourmet grocery store. It was amazing to watch blind students juggle their chef's knives, chopping boards, and table-top gas cookers. They were having such a marvelous time and I loved assisting and feeling useful again. Although my involvement with Janice was rewarding and we both realized that the Lord had orchestrated our meeting, I knew that this brief union would simply be a stepping stone. My incubation period would soon be coming to an end.

The Lord had quieted my energetic spirit. I was learning to rest, to wait upon Him, and to stand on His promises to finish the work of restoring the many losses I had experienced in my life. I had been set aside to drink deeply from His presence. I had been stretched! My capacity was much deeper now. Many doors had closed behind me, many superfluous things had been trimmed away. He had put some things into alignment. Everything in my past had this season in mind....."*for such a time as this*"! (Est. 4:14). Now He was about to begin to break through beyond my imagination. There would be a new assignment ahead.

A DOOR OPENS

That's when I received the LETTER FROM ARIA! As much as I had been anticipating new doors to open, her proposal came as a total surprise! Her letter read something like this:

Dear Mother,

I know that you have struggled since the loss of your school and moving to Florida. Konnor and I have discussed this matter at length and I have a serious proposal to present to you which I sincerely hope you will consider and accept.

A few years ago Konnor built a house inside the barn on our forty-acre property. Although we keep the house heated and cooled it is currently sitting there unoccupied. It is simply waiting for you!"

Her letter continued in what became a magnificent sales pitch! She ended what was a much longer letter by offering many opportunities this move would present to me. Was I reading this correctly? I had known a door was about to open but to go to Pittsburgh? To live next to Aria and Konnor? On their property? Wow! I had been praying for a deeper restoration between Aria and me; was this how it would happen? She seemed to want me to come!!

Her perfectly crafted sales letter finally came to an end. *"Please give this much thought, Mom. You would have no housing expenses as we make them all ready. It would allow us to build our relationship. I truly hope you will accept!"*

And she ended, *"Love, Aria".*

Prayer surely changes things! Our relationship had already seen much improvement, but this was beyond my expectation! The previous year Aria had been diagnosed with a serious illness which gave me a great excuse to rush to Pittsburgh to care for her like a real mother for a month at her home. Her vulnerable condition allowed me the rare opportunity of being her loving caregiver. There had been great progress at restoring years of misunderstanding.

Aria had worked diligently to achieve her dream of becoming an accomplished and respected physician. Her husband and two step-daughters adored her! She had put much effort into putting her painful past behind her. How she had blossomed! And I had such renewed respect for her.

We had begun to know each other more deeply, becoming much more comfortable with each other. When my landmark birthday rolled around she surprised me by taking me on a Caribbean cruise! What a marvelous time we had together, laughing like school girls as if there never had been any problems between us. I think we were both surprised at how much we enjoyed each other!! Our restoration didn't occur overnight. The wounds were far too deep! But much progress had already been made!

God's Word not only guided me but gave me the final nudge to accept Aria's generous offer. *"Enlarge the place of your tent, And stretch out the curtains of your dwellings; Do not spare. Lengthen your cords and strengthen your stakes. For you shall expand to the right and to the left... Do not fear, you will not be ashamed, Neither be disgraced......And you will not remember the reproach of your widowhood any longer"* (Is. 54:2-4 NKJV).

A million thoughts raced through my mind, but deep in my spirit, I knew that this was the door that I had been waiting to open. Instinctively I knew this move would be about healing the wounds from our past. I would go in faith believing my God would complete that which He had started. Although I had prayed and prayed that our relationship would someday be restored, never had I dreamed Aria would invite me to live on her property, with only a few steps between us! God works in such mysterious ways His wonders to perform!

CHANGE   By this time I surely was no stranger to change! Even as a young person God was preparing me to be flexible enough to flow with changes in my life. When I was growing up my family made several moves. The momentous move came just as I was ready to start ninth grade. My dad bought a beautiful resort on the Oregon coast which required a move out of state. I had just been elected girls' club president of my 1,000 member junior high school to become effective when the fall term started. This was a big honor for a young girl, one which embarrassed me not to fulfill. I felt that I let down my classmates. Then again there were two additional moves my senior year, the hardest of all school years for a student to move to another school. But I made two moves!

Looking back on those moves I see God's hand molding me to be flexible and to learn to make the best of things beyond my control. I have faced opportunities in my life requiring change which I had the grace to make because I had learned to embrace change when young; not to fear change, but to welcome it when I felt the change was God directed.

Why are so many people resistant to change when change is often the very step the Lord uses to move us into our destiny or to test our faith? When an opportunity arises many people look for any number of excuses to avoid change. The excuses take on various forms: *"I'm too old!", "I don't have the experience",* or *"I'm too shy!"* If the opportunity would require relocating another set of excuses surface. *"I could never leave my beautiful home; God gave it to me!"* or *"I wouldn't move away from my relatives!"* or *"In my family, none of us do that or go there!"'*

Some of the biggest blessings in my life came after submitting to changes that the Lord presented to me. What blessings might I have forfeited had I not agreed to make the moves He offered me; to pursue the vision He gave me to be an executive director of an American-based cosmetic company? What if I had listened to my insecurities and fears rather than make the move to Florida? What? And miss becoming Pastor Ken's *Vanguard* team? To miss the blessing of standing in the gap for him? To miss watching Timmy's early childhood and Zyon's emerging leadership as a young man? To miss drawing close to my lovely daughter-in-law?

Some of the illustrations in the bible set an example. Abraham was given a tremendous promise, but he was required to put action to his faith. He not only embraced change but in obedience, he began his journey uncertain as to where he was going. *"By faith, Abraham obeyed when he was called to go into the place which he would receive as an inheritance. And he went out not knowing where he was going"* (Heb. 11:8 NKJV).

As Jesus was assembling followers some couldn't leave some things behind. Their excuses held them back from being *'all in'!* One said, *"I can't go now. I must bury my father"* (Luke 59:-60). Another wanted to follow but lacked the faith to leave his parents behind (Luke 9:61) and yet another was ready and willing, having fulfilled a requirement of keeping the law, until Jesus told him to, *"Sell everything you have and give to the poor"* (Mark 10:21). His greed or lack of faith was the line in the sand for him. Their lack of courage to make the required change cost these men dearly. Change was the only obstacle to have kept them from being in the inner circle of the Lord Himself!

What about Lot? The angel of the Lord led him and his wife by the hand out of sinful Sodom toward a place of refuge. Mrs. Lot missed the blessing the Lord intended for her by looking back in disobedience, thus resulting in her being transformed into a dead pillar of salt. Lot, too, missed God's best because he lacked the faith to continue the journey with Abraham; rather he chose to reside in a cave. His fear of change, insecurity, and faithlessness cost him the blessings of God's best.

I could have stopped in my tracks and not begun the writing of this book. Or I could opt to walk by faith. The choice was always mine. One choice is the way of blessing and faith, the other choice is the path of least resistance, insecurity, and inertia. Dear beloved Reader, are you facing some possible changes in your life? Do your dreams require you to change something, to put aside your insecurity? As you step out on the path of faith God will be glorified and doors will open for you as you see your destiny fulfilled! Muster up your courage and take that step of faith.

GETTING READY   I made a quick trip to Pittsburgh to check out the barn to determine what I needed to bring and what I should leave behind. It was such fun to assign my designer's mind the challenge of making this space my new home. I recalled in amazement that many years ago as a young woman I dreamed of restoring a barn! Most of my furniture would stay with David and Juju, but with a few carefully selected pieces, artwork, and of course, my magnificent new grand piano, I would make this big old barn my retreat, my sanctuary!

When I returned to Florida I busied myself preparing for my upcoming move. There were friends to see one last time. I would attend my last bible study to say final farewells to special friends and to have them pray for my new venture! The leader of the meeting had keen prophetic gifting; his prayer and prophetic words for me were the powerful impetus and encouragement I needed! My Christian friends wished me well, showered me with their love and support, and bathed me in loving prayers for a blessed new chapter. I was confident that my new assignment would be beyond my imagination, full of God's blessing! My God would demonstrate His power through me and *"I would not be ashamed"* (Is. 54.4). People would look at me and know only God could have brought me here.

ENEMY ATTACK! The enemy of my soul could also read the signals that I was about to move into my destiny and that greater restoration would soon be giving God great glory. The devil comes to kill, steal and destroy! Those powerful prophetic words spoken over me a few days earlier must have threatened him because he showed up with fanfare to try to ruin everything!

I had been in the habit of literally dancing down the stairs every morning to announce my *'good morning'* to my household. Picture this scene as I waltzed down the stairs a few days before to my move to Pittsburgh. Suddenly, *"Oh, My Goodness! BUMP! BANG!! UGH! HELP! Someone pushed me!"* It did feel as if someone had shoved me down that stairway! I instantly plummeted down the flight of stairs uncontrollably helpless to stop myself!!! THUD! THUD! More powerful THUDS!!! I couldn't stop myself! As I continued to thump from stair to stair my back would aggressively be forced against the riser behind me, propelling me down another step and another all the way to the bottom! *"My head"*, I moaned! With each successive descent, the force of my fall made my head feel like it was exploding! I somehow made my way to the sofa in the family room surrounded by David, Zyon, and Timmy's chorus of sympathy, love, and concern. I had been so rattled and shaken! Despite broken ribs and a nasty concussion, I still had much packing to do to make ready for my move in only a couple of days. With Juju's kind assistance, we got the job done.

In Konnor's typically generous style he flew from Pittsburgh to drive us to Sanford. From there we boarded the auto-train to transport my Audi to Washington, saving us from driving a lot of miles between Florida and Pittsburgh. It was relaxing to sit in the car's passenger seat enjoying the scenery amidst fleeting thoughts of the past chaotic week. Just as we were about to arrive at the train station, however, while stopped at a traffic light...<u>another catastrophe</u>!!! CRASH!... BANG! CRASH! Are you kidding me? Unbelievably, the vehicle directly behind us failed to stop at the light! <u>REAR-ENDED!</u> By a large fishing truck! *"I cannot believe it!"* That seemed like the last straw!

Eventually, we were finally seated on the train, my Audi neatly boarded in its own special compartment. Thankfully, the past was behind us. Although the constant jostling of the train on its tracks continued to rattle my injured brain, we would soon be in Pittsburgh to embark on my new assignment. What a tumultuous past few days!

I stayed in Aria and Konnor's home for nearly a month while finishing touches were being applied to the barn. One morning they both approached me saying that it was time to take me to the nearest hospital for x-rays; my lingering headaches were a growing concern! Never would I have imagined that those x-rays would result in my being rushed by ambulance to a large Pittsburgh hospital... for a craniotomy! Those ugly films of my brain largely shaded in black revealed ... I was having a serious Brain Bleed!

The next thing I remember was being wheeled down the corridor in a gurney of what I later learned was one of the nation's finest hospitals for neuro-surgery! My physician, too, was considered one of the nation's best! Once again the Lord had positioned me with favor in mind!

That was the introduction to my new chapter in Pittsburgh.

CHAPTER 15

LIFE IN PITTSBURGH

MY NEW CHURCH   As I was being wheeled down the hospital corridor for surgery a young nurse popped her head out of a door and said, *"Remember me, Marjorie? You sat next to me in church last week. I am praying for you as you go into surgery!"* That meant so much to me! After my surgery, there were visits from several other church members and many cards, too. It was so comforting to know I all ready had a loving church family!

Aria had done her homework. She knew that for me to be happy in my new surroundings it would be essential that I find a church filled with the Holy Spirit, preferably not far from home. She had one picked out before I arrived, although ironically she still did not attend church herself! When she saw videos online of a small congregation with hands raised to the Lord in worship she said, *"This looks like a church for Mom!"* I had already attended two services the first month after arriving in Pittsburgh. The first step I took across the threshold of that sanctuary I knew in my spirit that this was my new church home!

SURGERY   It is just marvelous to know that the Lord will take any situation to show Himself strong. In the case of my brain surgery I experienced the peace of God unlike I had ever known. My hospital room became a sanctuary of God's love and Presence. My unbelievably rapid healing was miraculous and God got all the glory! No one could believe it! My pastor's wife, Pastor Cindy, whom I grew to love like a sister was one of my first visitors. She still talks about coming into my room the day following my surgery expecting to see me drugged and in misery, only to be completely shocked that I was sitting up in bed, alert, with my hair in order, fresh make-up applied and tubes coming out of my head! What a sight I must have been! (Yes, I still had hair. My surgeon only cut a tiny strip of hair to make his incisions which my part later covered. I was so thankful not to emerge from surgery bald!)

ARIA'S KINDNESS!   This was all a testimony to daughter Aria and her husband, Konnor. As a physician, she was amazed at my incredible recovery, as was Konnor! He was facing his own probable upcoming surgery with great apprehension and my experience encouraged him. I was so touched by Konnor's spending an afternoon with me in the hospital; bringing a gorgeous bouquet of my favorite cobalt blue Siberian iris from his garden. And Aria was lovingly by my side most of the time.

God used my situation as an opportunity for Aria to do what she did best; be in control and look after me. So often in the past, we experienced a role reversal. She liked to be in charge. And so with great appreciation I usually let her make the plans, organize and arrange the details. If the occasion called for it she would even make a spreadsheet. All of these were things she would do to help me. Her knowledge of medicine was extremely helpful. Not only did I have my excellent primary care physician and neuro-surgeon caring for me, but Aria with her outstanding experience as an internal medicine doc was there for me as well! Physician Jesus oversaw every detail! I was in such good hands and felt such security and peace.

Aria was in control in other ways, too. In addition to her fine medical counsel, she insisted on picking up the tab when we would go to lunch or breakfast. She was incredibly generous with me in every way. I said to her on more than one occasion, *"Aria, I would ordinarily feel so embarrassed by your paying for so many things for me. It just seems backward since I am the mother, especially because I am such an independent person."* This was a discussion I needed to bring up with her, to shed light on the subject. *"However, I understand that this is how you display your kindness and love for me in a manner that is comfortable for you. Although it is very humbling for me to receive, I accept it and am most appreciative and grateful!"*

It was true. I grew to accept the arrangement, believing the Lord Himself had written the script in exactly this way for Aria to feel confident and for me to be humbled! It was a win/win situation.

THE BARN/HOUSE   The Lord met all my needs. The barn-house was cozy and my eclectic collection of art and furnishings transformed the place. I fashioned yards and yards of "distressed" laundered painter's drop cloths into shabby chic draperies to soften the roughness of old barn boards and provide privacy. I made do in the make-shift kitchen by buying a stainless steel work table to compensate for the lack of counter space. A pot rack hung my pans conveniently within reach and an old potting table provided additional workspace. Finally I discovered a small bookshelf in the barn which, when placed on top of the countertop, became the open cabinet for my dishes and glasses! The unsightly laundry sink and water heater were quickly hidden behind my "shabby chic" draping in what now became my pantry with the addition of stainless steel shelving units. What my barn-kitchen lacked in modernity it made up for in "charm" and character!

My dining room space had slightly sloping floors which you didn't notice too much if you just kept in mind that this was in actuality *a barn!* I had moved my large old china cabinet with me which I would still need to house my china, linens, and silver. I found quite a shabby old picnic table in the barn that I usually kept covered with a French country cloth. There were times I would expose the rough wood and use chunky straw mats, linen napkins, and large rustic lanterns for soft light. Around the table were eight antique Spanish dining chairs I'd had for years which I moved with me from Arizona to Florida. They were one of a kind, had a pleasing scale and featured nail-heads, rope-twist legs, and leather seats and backs. Against the wall was my long contemporary rusticated steel and glass serving table with a large mirror above it. My old Oriental rugs made themselves right at home throughout the barn. Nothing matched, but somehow it all just fit in an eclectic sort of way!

Upstairs were two loft bedrooms. This created high two-story ceilings in the living room. On each of the two facing upstairs loft walls in the living room hung a pair of deer antlers which were a real "find" when I discovered them in the barn. I loved the sculptural form of the antlers, but more importantly, they reminded me of God's Word, *"He makes my feet like hinds feet and sets me on high places"* (Ps. 33:18) and *"As the deer pants for streams of water so my soul pants for you, my God"* (Ps. 42:1).

A BARN CAN BE A COZY PLACE TO LIVE

NOTICE THE ANTLERS

MY SUNNY ATRIUM

ANTIQUE CABINET AND ARTWORK

DRAPED DOOR IN MY LOFT

While arranging things in the barn, the Lord graciously was teaching me some things. As a professional interior designer with a long career behind me, I had rather specific ideas about how to put my house (barn) in order. There were some challenges to deal with, however. One, of course, was my limited budget. But more specifically was that this was not my property and I didn't feel very comfortable asking Konnor to make the changes I wanted. He had been so very kind and generous with me I surely didn't want to become an irritation. As time progressed I learned to simply trust the Lord with my (design) needs and desires, trivial as they were sometimes. Amazingly, the Lord would teach me to wait upon Him until the issue no longer seemed important, and then He would put it in Konnor's mind to make the change. This happened again and again. So the Lord and I partnered in the interior design of my barn/home.

MY NEW CAR   Another area where the Lord had proven Himself to be my provider was with my car. My Audi was part of my divorce settlement, but foreign automobiles are expensive to maintain. Since I had no mechanical ability at all, I was uneasy about my car mainte-nance. I took my car to Pep Boys probably way too often to have my oil checked, or some other minor condition I had a concern about. The boys there were just amazingly patient with me. Many times they would put in a quart of oil at no charge. Sometimes I would bring a box of delicious cookies to reward their kindness. The Lord was watching over me. As long as I owned that Audi, miraculously it never needed any repairs. Amazingly, the two flat tires I had were strategically both in front of tire stores!

After I had been in Pittsburgh awhile the Lord spoke to me very defi-nitely one morning as I awoke. What He put in my spirit surprised me. He said, *"It's time for you to look for another car. You have put enough miles on the Audi that there will need to be repairs soon and that will be too expensive for your budget. You need an American car now, Marjorie!"* Not even one time had I considered buying another car. Since the loss of my school and its accompanying foreclosures on my home and campus, I never imagined my credit would qualify me for an auto loan. I discussed the matter with Aria and in her usual take-charge style she immediately began searching for what she thought would be a practical vehicle for me. The used car lot owner worked out all the details to secure a loan.

With Aria by my side, we drove quite a distance fully prepared to trade in the Audi and drive home in my new car that she had carefully selected! Mr. Car Lot Owner had the vehicle all ready for me, but one look at it, and I was disappointed. It just wasn't my style! My Audi had spoiled me, I guess. But my eyes fixated on a snappy red Buick Encore with leather interior. I was assured that the upgrade wouldn't be a problem for me to still qualify for the loan. But first, of course, my car had to be test-driven. After the brief test-drive I was asked, *"How long has your Audi been shimmy-ing?"* I was shocked! *"What? I just drove 45 minutes and it certainly did NOT shimmy! I've never had a problem with it!"* I don't know if they believed me, but they decided to honor my deal anyway. After adjusting some numbers we were ready to close the sale, but the lender's computer shut down. Another glitch! *"Come back after the weekend. The loan will be secured and you may drive away in your new car then, Ma'am!"*

We headed home a little disappointed that we weren't driving the new car, but only had driven a few miles when the *shaking and wild, jerking movements* began! She was *shimmy-ing*!!! We limped back to the car lot to wait for Konnor to retrieve us. We would surely be back Monday to drive home in the Buick!

I loved the way the Lord instructed me that it was time to find another car before costly repairs strained my budget. He oversaw me all the way to the car lot before she broke down!!! All in His usual perfect timing! I know that whatever the mechanical problems were it would have been too expensive for me to pay for parts and service on my foreign luxury car. Even though I was very excited to have such a snappy new car, that excitement could not compare to the joy I felt that the Lord was taking such good care of me! He was writing the script for all my needs to be met!

THE LORD EVEN SELECTED MY NEW CAR!

It had been only two weeks after major surgery that I was back in my new church! I just couldn't wait to meet everyone and get back into church worship! The pastor gave me an invitation to testify of my brain surgery. The Word says *"They overcame him by the blood of the Lamb and the word of their testimony..."* (Rev. 12:11). It was quite satisfying to tattle on the devil that his efforts of pushing me down the stairs had backfired!

The ladies in the church kept telling me, *"You must meet June!"* She had been conducting women's bible classes with great passion and dedication for years. The ladies loved her. Before I even met her I knew we would connect! One of my first Sundays back to church I spied her and made a beeline to introduce myself to her. *"Yes, I conduct three classes on Thursdays and one on Fridays; back to back."* I was amazed at her vitality and energy and found myself responding, *"What? And you do all that without assistance?"* I immediately took the initiative of telling her that I had been a women's ministry leader in Tucson and had taught many women in my design school, hoping this would give me a little credibility. *"I am offering to help you in any way I can; wherever you may need me. Just put me to work."* June is one of those people who is very self-sufficient. She accomplishes more in one hour than most of us could do in a day. Amazingly she accepted my offer considering that she knew nothing of my background and had managed quite nicely without assistance thus far. She would naturally need to be cautious about who would assist her in her ministry. June's Bible classes became my mission field, too. I never felt that I did that much to assist her. June was just used to doing things for herself. But I showed up for classes every Thursday at 10:00 AM, noon, and 7:00 PM and again on Fridays at 11:00 AM. June had a style all her own of teaching the Word interspersing the lessons with her vivid personal experiences. She had a gift of making the bible come alive and ladies of various backgrounds and stages of maturity flocked to her meetings faithfully every week. The love of God knit our hearts together. We were family.

THE INFAMOUS JUNE!

CHRISTMAS WITH THE FAM   Christmas was coming and the whole family would be together! The first time in many years . ... Tim and Jeni from Thailand, David and Juju, Zyon and Timmy from Florida, and of course, Aria and Konnor. I was beyond myself with giddy preparations; meal planning, baking, stocking the freezer, and endless Christmas shopping. And of course, I would dress up the barn with fresh, fragrant greenery and a Christmas tree decorated with unbelievably beautiful ornaments given to me by my dear new friend. Many other friends rallied to help stock my larder and to help with the decorations...a real team effort to celebrate my family restoration!

The holiday was hectic, but blessed. We tried to cram years into a few days. We took turns with meal preparation in my tiny kitchen; each one had his/her specialty; Tim – Thai food, of course, Juju – Indian cuisine, Aria – anything gourmet, and David – homemade waffles! When we sat down around the table I would look at each one and get all teary-eyed knowing how far the Lord had brought us. I thought of all the tears shed for them and just marveled at my wonderful, grown-up children! My seed! God had blessed every one of them in different ways. I could just see God's hand resting on each of my children and grand-children. They were all unique and such a gift to my life!

OUR CHRISTMAS WAS SUCH FUN!

BROTHERS

COUSINS TIMMY & JENI

LOVELY JUJU

CROQUET AT CHRISTMAS

and THEN IT SNOWED!

When Paul and Silas miraculously were set free of their chains and the prison doors flew open the jailer insisted on knowing what he must do to be saved. *"Believe in the Lord Jesus and you will be saved—-you and your entire household!"* (Acts 16:31). Sometimes I would just call out the words *"You and your entire household, in Jesus name"* as a declaration knowing that my spoken words are powerful. When Zacchaeus believed in the Lord, Jesus said to him, *"Today salvation has come to this house because this man, too, is a son of Abraham."* As children of Abraham, through Jesus, we have received the promise of salvation for our entire family. I could rest on God's promises no matter how much unbelief my kids might have been in at any given time.

BACK PAIN   God had brought us closer as a family. His healing process was at work. But I was exhausted! My newly quiet lifestyle wasn't used to all that commotion! Just about the time that they all left, my back went out. This began the chapter of my life entitled *'Back Pain'!* Week after week became month after month of mounting back pain, frequent trips to various chiropractors, each one seeming to offer renewed hope. Tedious exercise. Physical therapy. More physical therapy. Pain patches and pills. Nothing helped.

ATTITUDE   I learned a lot during those months of pain. I continued helping June with the bible studies. Few ladies knew I was in such agony, even though I could not stand up straight. I would greet them with a smile at the door, gripping the nearby table, sitting down as much as possible.

I spent a lot of time lying on my bed. I learned that even in pain I could enjoy the life God gave me every day. I could still praise the Lord. I had so much for which to be thankful! I could call someone to encourage them. I could sing, I could read, I could pray, I could praise the Lord and I could surely still laugh! There were indeed many things I could still do. One thing I learned was that I could still have a good attitude. My days could be good days or bad days depending on my attitude. I chose to have a good attitude. I once heard that the main difference between prophetic people and pathetic people is their attitude. *"Life is 10% of what happens to you and 90% how you react to it!"* (Charles Swindoll).

I like what Abraham Lincoln so wisely said, *"We can complain because rose bushes have thorns, or we can rejoice because thorns have roses".*

I practiced trying to avoid referring to *'my bad back'*, *'my backache',* or *'my scoliosis'*, which only would become a prophetic curse. Why claim those conditions as *'mine'* when I was claiming healing? Wouldn't that be contradictory?

Although Phil. 4:8 (NKJV) had been a *'life verse'*, it now became even more pertinent as I considered, *"Finally, brethren, whatsoever things are true, whatsoever things are honest, whatsoever things are just, whatsoever things are pure, whatsoever things are lovely, whatsoever things are of good report; if there be any virtue, if there be any praise, think on these things".*

CHAPTER 16

SURGERY AND MORE

CRUISE   I began to pray about surgery. Would the Lord heal me in this manner? In the meantime, Aria arranged for us to take a Norwegian cruise together, just the two of us! We had the best time any mother/daughter could ever have together! Building memories! Our flight was scheduled to go from Pittsburgh to Detroit, change planes then go on to Amsterdam. Unfortunately, there was a long unexplained delay in the Detroit terminal followed by our flight being canceled. We had allowed a day in Amsterdam, so we did have a cushion of time. Aria, in her usual custom of being detail-oriented, would periodically ask me, *"Mom, do you still have your passport? Check your purse for your passport! I don't mean to nag, but would you just check for your passport one more time?"*

Fortunately, the airline provided lodging in the terminal hotel for the night. We were exhausted! Just to relieve Aria's anxiety I relented, tossing my passport onto her bed for safekeeping assuming she would put it in her purse where she could take control of guarding it. When she tossed the covers back before going to sleep, the passport inadvertently fell onto the floor on the far side of the bed just waiting for the drama which would surely unfold the next day!

The next morning before we left our room to get breakfast Aria echoed her concern about my passport one last time. In our exhaustion the night before neither of us recalled my giving it to her to keep. In shock,

216

I retorted, *"I can't believe it, Aria, it's not here!"* Without my passport, there would be no cruise for us! We spent hours reliving our steps from the previous night; going back to the hotel desk, our gate, the airport police, and the lost and found. After an exhaustive hunt, we decided to take one last look in our room. It must be there! I insisted that I had scoured the room already, thoroughly retracing my steps from the previous night. *"OK, even though I never went near the window or that side of the room, I will look there nevertheless."*

What? Are you kidding? There on the floor between Aria's bed and the window lay my recovered passport, looking up and smiling at me as if to say *"I knew you would find me"*

The most encouraging thing about the lost passport was that Aria asked me to pray about finding it. Over the years the Lord had answered so many of my prayers for her. At that moment I realized she must have recognized all along the power of mother's prayers. She and I had an unspoken agreement that neither of us would discuss religion or politics. That worked for us. So I agreed to pray. Nothing more was said about that, but we did find the passport!

Everything about the cruise was beyond our expectations. When we tried to open the door to check into our stateroom the door would not open. Upon further scrutiny, we discovered that our key had a different number on it than the room to which we were assigned. Our new assignment was two decks higher! We were shocked to discover that we had been upgraded to a much more luxurious room than the one Aria had purchased; with a deck twice the size of our previous room and with many more amenities including a private concierge/snack room just across the hall. There was no question, God had shown us undeserved favor!

By the time we finally boarded the cruise, however, my compromised back made it very painful to walk very much at all. Nevertheless, we managed to do some excursions with the help of a wheelchair. Nothing could daunt the good time we were having! I recall how much laughter we exchanged, which was just the medication I needed. *"A merry heart is good medicine"* (Prov. 17:22).

When two people laugh together, it creates a bond. Everyone loves to laugh and to associate with someone with whom they can freely laugh. Not only do the scriptures instruct us to have a joyful heart, but modern science has discovered many health benefits associated with laughter, too; decreased depression, improved memory, a bolstered immune system, and relief of stress and pain. So why not laugh? Viktor Frankl, a Jewish concentrate camp survivor, said: *"I would never have made it if I could not have laughed. It lifted me out of a horrible situation, just enough to make it livable".* Others had something to say about laughter.

> Ben Franklin: *"Trouble knocked at the door, but hearing laughter, turned away!"* Victor Hugo: *"Laughter is the sun that drives winter from the human face".* George Bernard Shaw: *"You don't stop laughing when you grow old, you grow old when you stop laughing!.* Jewish proverb: *"As soap is for the body so is laughter for the soul"!*

I am so thankful that I can laugh easily; most often at myself! My third-grade school teacher made a note of it on my report card, *"Marjorie has a cheerful disposition and a very contagious laugh!"* I believe God has a keen sense of humor, too. He has made that very obvious by the hilarious situations in which He has placed me again and again! We are more likely to laugh easily by maintaining a childlike attitude. I read that children laugh on an average of 150 times a day, whereas by the time a child reaches adulthood that figure has dwindled to a mere 12 times. How unfortunate. No matter how grim my situation ever became I am so very glad I always could laugh easily.

LUMBAR FUSION   With the cruise behind us I made a real effort to find out God's will as to treating my back. Although previous chiropractic treatments had been unsuccessful, I decided to give one more chiropractor a chance. After numerous adjustments, the chiropractor took me aside and said, *"Marjorie, I have done all I can do for you. Your situation is complicated. Here is the name of a highly regarded neuro-surgeon in Pittsburgh.*" Nobody wants to get news like that, but my trust was in the Lord. I would follow His lead. My prayers went something like this:

"Father, you formed me from my mother's womb. You also know the damage caused from my fall down the stairs. I am in Your able hands and I trust You for my complete healing. Your Word says that '...All may go well for me, even as my soul gets along well'" (3 John 2). *I am not going to dictate HOW you should heal me, I just believe that You will. If surgery is how You desire to heal then lead me to the right surgeon. Direct my path. May Your will be done, dearest Lord Jesus. I praise you for my healing. Amen".*

I knew that His Word proclaimed, *"...By His wounds we ARE healed"* (Is. 53:5), indicating that the healing had already been accomplished, but it just had not yet manifested. Perhaps He would use surgery in my case. He would make it clear.

I made the appointment to see the neuro-surgeon that had been recommended. One look at the films of my spine and he barked at me: *"There is no way I can help you! I'll refer you to a younger specialist. He might have 'tricks' that I don't!"* I guess he didn't have the 'trick' of having a bedside manner either. The difference between the two physicians was night and day. My initial conference with Dr. Hamilton convinced me to have the surgery as soon as possible. He was confident that he could straighten my misaligned spine. I knew that he had been hand-picked for me by the Lord. His specialty was trauma injuries and my fall down the stairs qualified me for that!

I had surrendered the situation to the Lord; as a result, I had perfect peace. I believed He would guide Dr. Hamilton's hands to heal me. I had believed the Lord for complete healing. If the best way for my healing to glorify Him was surgery, I was willing. This was the route God chose for my healing to manifest. With Aria at my bedside and knowing David and Juju were in Florida praying for me, I still hoped to hear from my Tim, in Thailand, before the surgery. Just as my gurney was about to be wheeled down the hall to the operating room to start the procedure his call came. Tears of mother-love emotion rolled down my face. I had heard from my son. I looked at Aria sitting by my side and mumbled between sobs, *"My kids!"* She understood. All was well. I was ready now for the operating table.

Dr. Hamilton had quite a task to align what the enemy had done by pushing me down the stairs. As a side benefit, my lifetime condition of scoliosis was also corrected through the surgery! Eight hours on the operating table and numerous screws, rods, and bone grafts later I had been given a new lease on life!

RESURRECTION SOUP   One day following my surgery an angel rescued me! I had lost quite a lot of blood during the operation requiring me to have numerous blood transfusions. Someone from the kitchen came into my room noticing that my lunch tray had scarcely been touched. Truly, I was too weak to eat. She promised to be back shortly with her special power stew that would indeed bring me needed strength! It sounded like she was going to the kitchen to whip up something just for me! In no time she was back in my room with a bowl of steaming hot soup. After only a few tastes I was certain that she must have been an angel! That soup was what I call *'Resurrection Soup'.* Life poured into me with each taste! From that bowl of soup onward, I was strengthened and restored!

BLESSED RECOVERY!   My recovery was nearly immediate! A few days later I returned to Aria's house where she would watch over me fulfilling her wonderful role as caregiver. I marvel at God's wonderful ways. He not only used the surgery to perfectly align my back but used it as a tool to deepen my relationship with my girl. Medicine was her forte. It was what she knew best. Now she was watching over me like an angel with the honed skills of an outstanding physician! And God gave me amazing, miraculous grace to sail through the healing process.

A side benefit of the entire situation was I discovered how many wonderful friends God had put into my life! Cards wishing me well with words of encouragement and prayers came from far and wide. So much food was prepared for me by my friends that I didn't need to do much cooking for months! And Aria continued looking over my shoulder as daughter/caregiver. I felt so blessed, so loved, and content. My cup runneth over!

SCARS   In time the only reminder I had of my surgery was the long, nearly invisible scar that embellished my backbone. Nearly all of us carry a scar story. A scar is a lingering sign of damage or injury, either mental, physical, or emotional. Every wound results in some degree of scarring. Scarring is an ingenious part of the healing process in which the body uses the build-up of scar tissue to protect itself, starting with a protective scab. My long spinal scar is an obvious reminder that is visible, but the inner, invisible wounds I have incurred in my emotions have been protected by scars of a sort, too. I can choose to relive those hurtful situations that once wounded me or opt to allow time to do its work of dimming those memories by creating a scab of healing.

Although the scar on my back is a reminder of the past surgery and pain, the wound it covers doesn't hurt anymore.

If we continue to pick at our outward scab, healing cannot manifest. Likewise, inner healing is impossible if we keep picking away at our hurts, rejection, betrayals, and wounds. Some wounds continue to fester because doubt, fear, and unbelief continue to keep the pain alive! But Jesus is always there to bear our burdens. He died for that very purpose so we wouldn't have to. We can be free by casting our cares upon Him. That means we must quit picking at those inner wounds and heartaches! If we leave our natural wound alone it will heal in time, just as our inner wounds will diminish in time as well. *"He heals the broken-hearted and binds up all their wounds"* (Ps. 147:3). That is such a wonderful promise! As we walk with Him He is faithful to compassionately heal us from walking out our lives in pain. Oh dear One, just start thanking Him for making you free, and do not dwell on those past hurts!

The memory of past losses which once caused me much pain, now serve to increase my compassion for others who suffer in a like manner. The wounds I once suffered have equipped me for service to the Lord. My wounds are healed, only a trace of a scar reminds me of past pain and that He brought healing. *"For He wounds, but He also binds up. He injures, but His hands also heal"* (Job 5:18 NKJV). He comes with *"Healing in His wings!"* (Mal. 4:2 NKJV)

Great victory and power usually come at a price, a price that leaves some scars. I am reminded of the words the Lord whispered to me in my Damascus Road experience, *"Have you counted the cost?"* I am fighting a good fight of faith to serve Him as I run the race of Life, a fight that admittedly inflicted a cost that has left a few scars. But one day I shall meet Him face to face. When I hear the words, *"Well done, good and faithful servant!"* it will be worth every wound and trial! All my scars will then be gone!

ZYON'S GAP YEAR AT THE BARN WITH ME   Zyon graduated from high school at only sixteen years old. He had skipped a grade as well as started school young. He chose to take a *'gap year'*; a year out of high school to mature and get ready for college. Having made that decision he opted to stay in the barn-house with me during that season. Zyon's college search became Aria's mission during those months as she diligently tutored him for upcoming SAT exams. She spent hours helping him select a small liberal arts school that would be just the right fit. They scheduled college tours and open houses, some of which I tagged along, too. He got his first job at a car wash and began to get a little taste of the world of finance starting with opening his own bank account.

I loved having Zyon stay with me. It was a golden gift from God. He had always been such a joy to me!

ZYON AT THE BARN WITH ME

RE-ENTER MILTON   During those months in Pittsburgh there had been another unexpected surprise. Just before leaving Florida, I found it necessary to contact Milton about a business matter. Before ending the conversation he went in another direction. He rather timidly began, *"I've had time to consider events from the past. I have a lot of regrets. After the loss of the school , I just had sort of a break-down. Truthfully, God has truly humbled me. Do you think we could be friends now?"*

I certainly did not expect to hear that! This seemed to be a different Milton! I responded cautiously, *"Milton, I forgave you a long time ago and have moved on. When you and I married you stepped into my life... my family, my career, my home. Our marriage started in the wrong order of things. Yes, you and I can be phone friends. But that's all. Unless you are in a secure financial position our relationship could not go any further."* I laid down the ground rules. I did not want to become emotionally involved again only to be disappointed, so we agreed that it would be a phone friendship only.

Thus, he and I became phone friends and God healed the hurtful wounds of our broken marriage. Over the next few months, we began to understand one another more fully. God used those phone calls to heal shattered emotions in both of our lives and furthered the restoration process that God had promised. Now, one more piece of the mosaic of my life was unexpectedly put into place!

CONTENTMENT   With the move to Pittsburgh, a new church, family relationships restored and growing deeper and two major surgeries behind me I have a sense that the best is yet to come! It is marvelous to be in my golden years in such good health and be pain-free at last. I continue to embrace every day the Lord gives me. He has brought me a long way in teaching me to rest in Him, to live in His presence, and bubble over with thankfulness. When the world around me is in turmoil, I live in peace that the world doesn't understand. It passes understanding. Like Paul, I can say, *"I know what it is to be in need, and I know what it is to have plenty; I have learned the secret to be content in every situation whether well fed or hungry, whether living in plenty or want. I can do all this through Him who gives me strength!"* (Phil. 4:12-13)

A G I N G G R A C E F U L L Y   When I woke up one day after a milestone birthday I surprised myself with the shocking revelation that, *"My goodness, I am getting old!"* I didn't know how to do "Old"; I had no experience in it. I don't think like an old person and surely do not feel like it! My kids are even getting old. Yet my calendar confirmed it. My youth has long since been swallowed up! Who is that staring back at me in the mirror? May these secrets to "aging gracefully" bless you on your journey!

<u>Clearing The Way (abridged)</u>

I have waited quite a long time to get old, so I think I should try to enjoy it. I can't turn it in for a refund and I surely don't want to destroy it.

I would like to lighten the luggage I've accumulated over the years.
I'd be smart to release all the memories that brought about heartache and tears.

That would make living much better, free up space that then could be filled
With appreciation for the good things in life, with the promise that
then I could build

A future that lives for the moment with little concern for the past.
My time will be filled with contentment, no matter how long it will last.

By Alora M.

Some secrets I have discovered to enable me to age gracefully:

1. Fill one's days with the Lord's presence and one's mouth with
   His praises
2. Always have a word of encouragement for someone at my
   fingertips
3. Be ready to laugh at all times

As I follow this formula the joy of the Lord becomes my constant
strength, His peace indeed passes all understanding and His Life sustains me with inner strength. The body may be getting older, but the
spirit is energized, full of Life!

Just as in all of life, our days will be meaningful if we have a purpose. In
my career days, there were never enough hours in the day. I had plenty
of purpose, but life was often hectic as I ran three businesses at once.
Now that I am retired I have more time, but what is my purpose?

INTERCESSION   I found a wonderful purpose to carry me
throughout my senior years, no matter how feeble my body may become.
I have become an intercessor! This is a purpose with eternal dividends
which will affect many people, even nations! I belong to zoom phone
intercessor groups as well as to my church women's weekly intercessory
group. We have bonded in the spirit and in purpose, eagerly waiting

for Wednesday evening so we might rock heaven with our praise and petitions.

We are learning to become mighty in our intercession, saying goodbye to our anemic *nicey-nice* prayers of former days. As we declare and decree the Word of God, wielding the sword of the spirit and using the authority the Lord has given us, we often see incredible results of our prayers. When He directs us to pray for something He is just waiting for us to speak His will into the atmosphere so it may be done on earth as it is in heaven! Jesus taught us to declare *"Thy kingdom come and Thy will be done on earth as it is in heaven"* (Matt. 6:10); to use our voices to loose heaven's blessings on to the earth. We can declare righteousness and justice to be loosed on earth as they already are in heaven *("righteousness and justice are the foundation of His throne"* Ps.89:14). There are so many scriptures we can decree over the earth to bring about change, restoration, and blessings!

It is an amazing thing to consider that our God of the universe, who had the power to put the stars in place, has chosen to use our mouths to pray for the miracles He wants to perform! Just imagine! We can co-partner with God Almighty!

We take the Word of God seriously when it comes to intercession, realizing that we *"Wrestle not against flesh and blood, but against principalities and powers in heavenly places"* (Eph. 6:12). Satan, who came to lie, steal and kill, doesn't miss an opportunity to do what he does by wreaking havoc wherever he goes. But the Lord gave us authority to wage war on him and his demons by applying the blood of Jesus and calling upon the powerful name of Jesus. We have the authority to bind the enemy, to cast him out, and to demand he set the prisoner free. We can cancel his assignments and nullify his power, rendering him weak and ineffective! The last words Jesus spoke on the cross were *"It is finished"*! (John 19:30). He did it all! Now we are left with the responsibility to learn how to fight the good fight with victory! We win! Jesus *always causes us to triumph!* (2Cor. 2:14 KJV).

The Hebrides revival in the late 40s and early 50s illustrates the power of prayer. Sisters Peggy and Christine Smith, one blind and the other crippled with arthritis, were in their eighties and too infirmed to even attend church. Yet, their compromised conditions did not dilute the power of their prayers which impacted thousands. They prayed night and day for revival to come to their home town in the Hebrides Islands reminding God of His promise to "...*Pour water upon him who is thirsty and floods upon dry ground. I will pour my spirit upon your Descendents and on your offspring*" (Is. 44:3). Indeed revival came to hundreds and especially impacted young people. What purpose those two sisters carried as their prayers moved the heart of God. What if they had not answered that call to intercede?

WISDOM   Plato said, "*Wise men speak because they have something to say; fools speak because they have to say something!*" So many situations in my life have provoked me to request the Lord's wisdom. He has been faithful to His Word to "*Provide wisdom generously*" (James 1:5). All of that wise counsel over the years has built an arsenal of 'sense' and 'know-how', now at hand for me to share with younger less mature believers. "*Is not wisdom found among the aged? Does not long life bring understanding?*" (Job 12:12).

Wisdom is teaching me not only what to say, but what not to say. Tied very close to wisdom is timing. A sure ingredient of wisdom is knowing when to apply it. Sadly, by the time one finally acquires wisdom others often are inclined to ignore it thinking that the old fool is too old to know anything! Or an annoying bout of forgetfulness makes it hard to recall that treasure chest of wisdom we have stored up through our years of experience.

Just as aging has produced an accumulation of wisdom, so has my trust in the Lord grown stronger as the years have passed. He has proven Himself to be trustworthy over and over. I do not just hope He will come through for me, but I just know that He will. Time has done its work.

The scriptures tell women what to do with that wisdom. Titus 2:3-7 tells older women to *"Urge the younger women to love their husbands and children, to be self-controlled and pure, to be busy at home and to be kind, and to be subject to their husbands so that no one will malign the word of God".* There is such a need today for Godly wisdom to be shared with a younger generation that has been so strongly influenced by an ungodly world system. Sometimes I will invite a young lady to my home for tea. The conversation invariably turns to sharing stories that provide Godly counsel to her.

Young men today, also, need Godly role models. *"Encourage the young men to be self-controlled. In everything set them an example by doing what is good. In your teaching show integrity, seriousness, and soundness of speech that cannot be condemned, so that those who oppose you may be ashamed because they have nothing bad to say about us!"* (Titus 2:8). So many young men today need wise counsel from a Godly man; many that have grown up without a father in their lives.

PARING DOWN   As I have grown older I have rid myself of superfluous baggage. This includes habits and mindsets, including that old demon of perfectionism! I believe in carrying a sense of excellence, but perfectionism is *excellence in excess.* This makes life stressful. I am learning that good is *good enough.* I realized it was time to say *'Good-bye'* to Super-Woman! I have had many lady friends that also suffer from perfectionism which will often rear its ugly head when we entertain. How many holidays were we driven by perfectionism to decorate, bake and clean with obsession only to be spent and exhausted when the big day arrived!

When I moved to Florida I found it necessary to pare down my belongings. I always loved beautiful things! Especially if they were shoes! Having been in the design industry I was constantly around beautiful furnishings and accessories. When I lost my school my home became the showcase for many of these items. But there came a time to say good-bye to sentimentality. Again when I moved to my barn/home in Pennsylvania another purging was required. Getting rid of a lot of stuff I had collected over the years has made life much simpler. The de-cluttering has lightened my life. Simpler is liberating. I had to come to grips with who owned whom? Did I own my things or did they own me?

THE INTERNET   What a tool the internet can be for us to keep in touch and send a little smile to others. It takes so little time to send an e-card or e-mail to a shut-in, or just to encourage someone we care for. This is a marvelous way to let our light shine. We can send a little message to a grandchild just to keep in touch. When my darling granddaughter, Jeni, was younger I used to mail a card or letter to her in Thailand often just to keep in touch. In each envelope I would put a trinket of some sort to remind her how special she is to me...a scarf, a bracelet, a piece of candy, or a stick of gum. I once sent her a letter made up completely of words and pictures from magazines. She became a teenager and rather outgrew that mode of communication, but I can still send an email.

A VESSEL FOR THE HOLY SPIRIT   I have a conviction that because I carry the Holy Spirit I want to look my best to honor Him. My outward vessel represents the Holy Spirit. What kind of a testimony is it to represent the Holy Spirit looking shabby and being poorly groomed or dressed? I try to take care of my appearance; exercise, eat properly, take my vitamins and supplements, have a skin-care routine, and maintain good grooming. I have finally traded wearing those high heels for medium-heeled shoes. Just because I am older does not mean that I cannot be fashionable! When I was about to have back surgery I asked my surgeon if I would still be able to wear high heels. I faced surgery willingly when his answer was, *"I am all for it!"*

GRANDCHILDREN   Oh! To be a grandparent! One of the greatest joys of being older is having grandchildren. What joy they bring us. We can relive childhood all over again with another generation; our seed. How fun to play again! To bake with the grandchild, to read a story to him, and especially to deposit truth and the Word into their lives! *"Even when I am old and gray, do not forsake me, my God, till I declare your power to the next generation and your mighty acts to all who are to come"* (Ps. 71:18). As a grandparent, we have a special privilege to leave our legacy behind in their young, impressionable lives.

MY SEED
TIMMY

JENI

ZYON

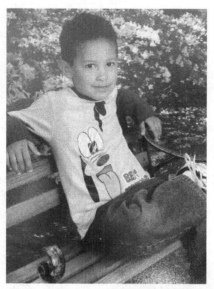

PRESSING ON   Having survived two major surgeries in less than two years as well as having experienced major losses, I could relate to Paul's comment about *pressing on*. *"Forgetting what is behind and straining toward what is ahead, I 'press on toward the goal to win the prize for which God has called me heavenward in Christ Jesus' "* (Phil. 3:13b–14).

That word, *'Press on'* caught my attention! That's what we do while we wait for our prayers to be answered, our breakthrough to possess what Christ has for us! I had been through the refining process. *'For such a time as this'* was the season I was approaching. I would *press on* with anticipation, hope and expectation. I press toward the goal for the prize of the upward call of God.

Each of us has a special design that is imprinted in our DNA which is uniquely ours! *"For you formed me in my inward parts; You covered me in my mother's womb...My frame was not hidden from You when I was made in secret. ...Your eyes saw my substance, being yet unformed. And in your book they all were written, The days fashioned for me, When as yet there were none of them"* (Ps. 139:13-16 NKJV). This explains why we are sometimes restless...we are waiting to experience that for which we were created.

So I press on.

I have lived my life pressing on. I have experienced valleys and mountains, ups and downs. Like Paul I have gained Christ! *"...I have suffered the loss of all things and count them as rubbish that I might gain Christ"* (Phil. 3:8 NKJV). Many material things which once mattered are insignificant to me now.

As I press on, I press in, not plow through. The best is yet to come.

STORY OF JEPHTHAH   The day I signed an agreement with my publisher to print my story, God spoke to my heart through a message I heard preached by my dear prayer-partner, former pastor, and dear friend, Pastor Ken Hughee. He has a tremendous gift of discovering revelation in the Word. It was appropriate that God would use his spoken Word to minister to me since I had partnered in prayer with Ken for years believing God would gloriously manifest the vision he was carrying. I had stood in the gap for him and had been his Vanguard team! Now God was using him to encourage me!

This message was a poignant story from Judges 11 about a bible character named Jephthah. Verse one begins by saying that Jephthah was a *"mighty man of valor"*. Immediately after making this bold claim, it surprisingly adds that *"He was the son of a harlot"*, two almost incongruent statements. Then, almost as an afterthought, the next statement says, *"And Gilead begot Jephthah"* (Judges 11:1). These statements oddly appear to be in reverse order according to human logic. Obituaries and eulogies traditionally begin with the birth of a person to his parents, followed by what he or she accomplished in life. We don't end with conception and birth! However, just as God called Jeremiah a prophet to the nations before he was even born, God called Jephthah to be a warrior for His people before conception! Jephthah's identity was that he was a *"mighty man of valor"*. It was simply his genetics that labeled him *"son of a harlot"*. *"God knew him before he was formed in his mother's womb"* (Ps. 139:15). That is who God called him to be; how He saw him! It was his destiny and purpose, his DNA. That explains why it is written first that he is a *mighty man of valor!*

Knowing that an individual will generally take the path of least resistance and be prone to human pride, God would need to orchestrate the circumstances in Jephthah's life to bring him to his destiny; so He ordained him to be the son of a harlot. It was the difficulties he faced that would build the character and strength necessary for the purpose God had designed for him.

After Jephthah's father, Gilead, had sired Jephthah with a harlot he raised him among the sons of his wife. But when his wife's sons were grown, they drove Jephthah out of the family home, saying he would have no inheritance. He moved to a distant city, saddened that he no longer had his brother's companionship or family ties. He just wanted to enjoy family life and be accepted by them. He had no aspirations for greatness; consequently fell into bad company. Having no means of support, he became a raider; otherwise known as a bandit!

It was during this wilderness time that Jephthah discovered the warrior in himself! Not only did he become a skilled fighter, but others recognized his leadership abilities and joined themselves to him. This was just in time for an elevation into his divine purpose. God was moving!

When the evil kingdom of the Ammonites decided to attack Jephthah's homeland of Gilead, the elders discovered that they had no one skilled in warfare to lead them into battle. So, they sought out Jephthah asking him to be their military leader. Not wanting to be used for their own purposes just to win their battle, Jephthah demanded that he also become the head of not only the military but leader over all of Gilead, including the elders. Suddenly, the man who only wanted a small plot of land as his inheritance was given the entire land. He had become the mighty man of valor that God always said he was! He overcame his humble beginnings and achieved his God-given purpose!

It made sense. Jephthah's life of difficulties and suffering molded him into God's masterpiece. His struggles and shame were the very tools God used to equip him to become a *mighty man of valor*. Jephthah would have gladly settled for far less, but the circumstances of his life elevated him beyond his expectations. The price he paid for his destiny to be fulfilled God's way was costly, but the results were powerful!

My life carries some parallels. I have surely risen above the aspirations I had as a young woman; to be a wife and mother. God allowed the circumstances of difficulties, loss, and shame to become my School Master. It took brokenness for me to be shaped into God's mosaic Masterpiece! Even so, faith tells me that the best is yet to come!

May God get the glory as He continues to fashion me into 'His Masterpiece'!

CHAPTER 17

KEYS FOR A VICTORIOUS LIFE

started writing this book as a legacy for my children and grandchildren that they might see the blessings of the Lord that followed me and that they would desire the same for their own lives. As time progressed I felt that my story might encourage others, too. So to all my dear Readers, I pray that you, too, will desire a deeper walk with Jesus as a result of reading how He has brought me such fulfillment, love, and joy.

In this my last chapter I am compelled to share some of the keys that have unlocked a victorious life for me. I am surely not the same woman that embarked on this journey many years ago. There have been forks in the road, steps of faith, losses, refiner's fires, successes and failures, a lot of waiting on the Lord! The Lord has been very patient with me, One with whom patience has not come easily. He has become my Life, my Love, my strength and courage, my peace, my hope.

May each of you grow in the grace and knowledge of the Lord Jesus Christ as you travel your journey. I trust some of my words have blessed you.

KEY OF FORGIVENESS   The word *"forgiveness"* is mentioned in the Old Testament thirteen times and once in the New Testament. The concept of forgiveness is mentioned much more frequently. *"Forgive"* is mentioned 42 times in the Old Testament and 33 times in the New

Testament. God must have felt it important for us to forgive. In my own life, it has been a major key to health, joy, liberty, and freedom.

First of all, we must come to Jesus and ask for His forgiveness for our sins. That is the very first step. He is the only way to the Father. *"...No man comes to the Father except by me"* (John14:6).

We must be quick to forgive others, too. My life was disrupted, shaken, and devastated when my husband left me and turned my children against me because of my faith in God. My world went topsy-turvy! I had every reason to be bitter and angry. I had been betrayed, emotionally battered, and bruised. It wasn't fair! I had been a good wife and mother. But, by the grace of God, I knew that hanging on to my broken heart, vengeance, anger, bitterness, and shame I would forever be the victim and he would go free. In forgiving my husband for the pain he caused me I would be free, liberated from grudges and bitterness. The pain of losing my children remained a long time, but God's grace guided me to forgive. It was a gift to me, too. By forgiving I avoided many consequences of hanging on to unforgiveness. And God has brought much restoration over the years.

61% of all cancer patients have forgiveness issues, more than half are severe (Dr. Michael Barry, *"The Forgiveness Prophet"*). Studies have shown that carrying unforgiveness can result in high blood pressure, depression, anxiety and lead to other illnesses, as well.

An unforgiving spirit separates us from fellowship with God. Sin will lead to guilt and shame, which in turn impairs our walk with the Lord. *"If someone says 'I love God but hates his brother, he is a liar...'"* (1 John 4:20).

By carrying unforgiveness one becomes bitter. The greatest enemy of living in joy and hope is the cultivation of bitterness. Bitterness moves you to a place you never wanted to be. You think dwelling on that issue will make you *better*, but instead, you become *bitter!* New relationships are sure to be infected by the poison of unforgiveness. By not forgiving and frequently thinking of that offense, a door often opens to a growing root of bitterness which can result in a miserable life and is not easy to eliminate.

Hope takes root in the soil of forgiveness but is lost in the atmosphere of unforgiveness and bitterness. *"Hope deferred makes the heart sick..."* (Prov. 13:12). *"Hope deferred"* is depression.

Research has shown that parent's unresolved issues pass on to their children. The feuds and hatred of people and families who cling to bitterness and unforgiveness are evidence of the tenacity of sin and its transmission from father to son. Attitudes, words, and actions pass on to your children.

If you, my Friend, have issues of hanging on to grudges or bitterness and unforgiveness, shed that weight immediately. Spare yourself all the miserable consequences that unforgiveness carries. Seek forgiveness from the Lord and the one that hurt you! You will breathe better and instantly be free from deadly weight! Victory will be yours.

Mark Twain must have tasted the fruit of forgiveness when he penned, *"Forgiveness is the fragrance that the violet sheds on the heel that has crushed it!"* When we forgive we cast all previous thoughts of *"getting even"* aimed toward the one who hurt us to the Lord who is a Master at dealing with our revenge issues.

One day in Pittsburgh Aria and I had a long wait together in a doctor's office. With time on our hands she had an idea, *"Mom, while we are waiting I can look up anyone from your past to see what they are now doing with their life if you like. I have this app..."* This sounded like an interesting way to pass the time! My mind went back to the loss of my school and specifically to the man responsible for closing me down; the former president of my school's regulatory agency in Arizona. Imagine my shock when the information she un-earthed hit me, *"My gracious! Are you ready for this, Mom?"* Her discovery rocked me! *"It seems that he died not too long after you lost the school!"* Immediately I thought of two scriptures, *"It is mine to avenge, I will repay. In due time their foot will slip...Their day of disaster is near and their doom rushes upon them"*

(Deut. 32:35) and also, *"Do not touch mine anointed Ones..."* (I Chron. 16:22 NIV).

God had avenged me. Although I had suffered tremendous loss at the hand of this man, the Lord had continued to bless me and meet all my needs, yet that former school board president reaped his costly due reward through the consequences of the grave. By forgiving him and others who had betrayed and hurt me, I moved on liberated and free, and in good health! I cannot emphasize enough how forgiveness is a major key to a blessed life of victory, health, and freedom! To forgive is to set the prisoner free, then realize that the prisoner is YOU!

Time and again the Lord has fought my battles and vindicated me as I put my enemies in His able hands. Another example involved the person that directed my cultural tours in Mexico for a while. Had the Lord not intervened this case could have ruined my business and reputation! Shopping expeditions in converted Spanish Colonial mansions were regular features my tours offered. However, this man began directing some of the tourists to local craftsman, on my dollar, yet retained the profit for himself. That wouldn't have been so bad, but I discovered that he pocketed $40,000 clients earmarked for custom kitchen cabinets that he didn't deliver. This left me responsible for his debt since it occurred on my tour. By this time he had moved to Mexico, opened a design business/showroom housed in a charming historic mansion. My attorney's sympathetic words to me were sobering, *"Since he is no longer living here in the States your hands are tied. I am so sorry for you, Marjorie. He took advantage of you in a big way! But you are now responsible."* He was serious when he added, *"Do you want me to see to it that his legs get broken?"*

What a horrifying comment! My response to him was that I would ask God to avenge me instead!

I was dumbfounded but certainly did not want to bring him harm. I had cared for him. I thought we were friends! How could he have taken such advantage of the opportunity I had given him? I had been betrayed! With the clients breathing down my neck I petitioned the

Lord. *"Lord, restore to me what the enemy has stolen. He is a thief and a robber! I decree 'Restoration' and demand that the devil loose every dime he stole. I declare that a spirit of conviction will torment my former employee night and day until the debt is paid in full".* To which I added, *"I give you thanks ahead of time for answering so thoroughly, my wonderful Lord!"*

I was thrilled to convey the good news to my attorney not too long afterward that not only did God hold my client's wrath at bay for a season, but my debtor repaid his debt in full, with apologies! God is so wonderful and always causes us to triumph when we trust Him!

KEY OF SELF-FORGIVENESS   I learned to forgive others before it became clear to me how important it was to forgive myself, too. The first step was to recognize my wrong. *"You shall know the Truth and it shall set you free"!* (John 8:32). It took time for me to realize that my children may have had some legitimate reasons to have been angry with me. More than anything I wanted them to understand the love of God and know of His ways. I had been zealous. Perhaps too zealous. It was painful to consider that the thing I wanted most to share with them would be the very thing that separated us. I must have done it all wrong. I shed many tears over my failures. The deepest goal of my life was to be a good mother, so any hurt I caused my children came back to haunt me again and again. I couldn't change what had been done. I would have to learn to forgive myself. In time I asked my adult children's forgiveness, too.

I was remorseful and humbled. Guilt and shame would attack me, but they were lies from the devil. I would become free as I discovered what God's Word had to say about my guilt and shame; that I had been forgiven and my sins were as far as the east is from the west. If my sins were buried why should I resurrect them? I could not change what had happened in the past, nor did my past failures define me. That was gone forever. I would forgive myself, not wallow in self-pity, and by God's grace move on. Self-forgiveness restores dignity. It was a process.

In an earlier chapter of this book, I wrote of a bleak period of several years in my life in which there was only silence between Aria and me. This followed her announcement to me that her anger didn't allow for any relationship between us at all. I tried to reconcile, but she wasn't ready. I cast my cares upon the Lord one hundred percent realizing that I couldn't undo the past, but with His grace, I could endeavor to be all I could be and let Him bring about the healing as I waited for Aria to receive me again. I had to learn to forgive myself, LET GO, and accept His forgiveness. The grace God gave me during that period was incredible! He brought many young women into my life with whom I ministered motherly wisdom and love; students and women's ministry ladies. God used that season to hone me into a vessel of honor. I would let go of my human pride, repent and allow His Word to direct me to not harbor self-pity, rather MOVE ON in faith. As I released my daughter into God's able hands, He worked in her life, too. I had more to learn about waiting upon the Lord.

He dug out such compassion within me for all those who have broken relationships in their families. Dear Reader, if that is you just cast your care on the Lord, receive His forgiveness for your role in that brokenness and trust in His many promises. If someone wronged you go to them and tell them you forgive them, too. Let forgiveness "rain" over you like a rainstorm and let it "reign" as it governs your life! Demonstrate that you believe Him by thanking Him for the answers and declaring restoration over your family. He never-ever fails and wants the best for you. He is our Way-Maker, Deliverer, Restorer and Healer of broken hearts. His Word tells us that *"...He bottles every tear..."* (Ps. 56:8 KJV). Isn't that beautiful! There must be lots of tear-bottles in heaven filled with Mothers' tears; including a closetful with my name on them that I have shed for my own beloved children!

Psalm 34:18-19 delivered such hope and comfort to me at times when the trials were heavy, *"The Lord is close to the broken-hearted and saves those who are crushed in spirit. The righteous person may have many troubles, but the Lord delivers him from them all!"* What a powerful promise!

KEY OF FELLOWSHIP   One of the greatest joys of my life has been the fellowship of Christian brothers and sisters. My Christian friends have been the seasoning in my life; the salt, the sugar, and zest! *"Forsake not the assembling of ourselves together as the manner of some is, but exhorting one another and so much more as you see the Day approaching"* (Heb. 10:25 KJV). Yes, the scriptures do instruct us to go to church.

"How good and precious it is to dwell in unity with the brethren..." (Ps. 133:1 NKJV). It is there in that place of unity with our brothers and sisters that *"the Lord commanded the blessing—-Life forevermore"!* (Ps. 133:3 NKJV). Each believer carries a portion of the Lord Jesus. With each relationship I see yet another facet of Him, always bringing me to a deeper appreciation of His diversity and beauty.

Some exceptional people have become my friends because I initiated the friendship. When I met my friend Cherry she and her husband were visiting my church. I greeted her and asked her to be my guest for lunch that week. That meeting was the beginning of a lifelong friendship. The bible has a suggestion for making friends. It says if you want friends you must *"show yourself friendly"* (Prov. 18:24 NKJV). I shudder to consider how empty my life would have been had I not cultivated friendship. It necessitates making an effort to initiate a friendship, but also to keep the friendship alive; fostering and kindling the flame of friendship is well worth the effort it requires.

When my children were young I used to sing to them a song which has stood the test of time as they still sing it: *"Make new friends; keep the old. Some are silver and some are gold".*

"Iron sharpens iron so one person sharpens another" (Prov. 27:17). Sometimes we need a word of correction to move forward. When iron sharpens iron, two implements are required. If the friend is acting in God's perfect timing and his word is gentle and kind it will be an easy pill to swallow, but that word needs to find a humble spirit in which to be deposited. I pray that I will always be humble enough to receive correction from a trusted friend. I also pray that I will be obedient when

the Lord's prompts me to be the iron to sharpen my friend's spirit and that I will have the sensitivity to wait upon Him for His perfect timing.

"Confess your faults to one another and pray for one another that you might be healed" (James 5:16). When we have a fault, failing or sin in our life the last thing we want to do is confess it to anyone. Our natural tendency is to keep it locked up in our inner being so we appear to be "good". But, that is a place of bondage; a prison of sorts. Our pride finds it embarrassing to admit to our failures. But, if we humble ourselves by confessing that problem to a trusted friend, the bible says *we might be healed*. The Greek word for *"confess"* is to speak it out loud, declare or actually blurt it out! When we confess that ugly sin or mental lie that has been tormenting us it is exposed; it is out in the open. Light always dispels darkness. A true friend is valued to keep us in check! If we are struggling with a weakness it can be so helpful to have a friend to whom we can be accountable; to confess our progress regularly until that sin is completely gone.

We were never meant to be alone. Although we surely cast our burdens on the Lord, in His kindness He provides friends along the way to give us support. There is nothing like a Christian friend to be there to *"carry one another's burdens..."* (Gal. 6:2). When I am burdened, I feel a heavy weight on me. It becomes difficult to carry. But when my friend helps carry that burden my load is lighter. I am relieved. Thank God for a true Christian friend.

"...One will chase a thousand, two will put 10,000 to flight..." (Duet. 32:30 NKJV). This is an amazingly powerful mathematical formula having to do with our spiritual warfare in the demonic realm, implying that there is power in numbers! The atmosphere is dominated by Satan and his demons. He is the *"Prince of the power of the air"* (Eph. 2:2 NKJV) and rules in the second heaven or in the atmosphere above us. When we pray we invade the atmosphere with our words. That breakthrough is all the more probable if several people are praying! As church members we have prayer warriors at our disposal to help empower us to fight the battles of life.

There are all kinds of friends. I have had friends that have been there for a season. They fill a need for awhile. We enjoy one another but changes occur in life and as time passes that person drops out of my immediate sphere of influence. There are a smaller number of friends, fewer than a handful, that are God's gift to me for life. Those friends might be separated from me by time and distance, but when we re-connect we are able to pick up again right where we left off. What a God-gift is a lifetime friend!

The bible speaks of a lifetime friendship between David and Jonathan; a friendship so strong that they made an oath to be friends in the name of the Lord between themselves and one another's descendants. This covenant was so strong that when Jonathon died David faithfully took on the responsibility of raising his crippled son, Mephibosheth, who became *"like one of the king's sons, even dining at his table"* (2 Sam.9:11 KJV).

Jonathan and David came from different backgrounds and had nearly thirty years the age difference between them. Their friendship was not a likely connection, rather one that the Lord himself orchestrated! Jonathan was of the tribe of Benjamin; David, the tribe of Judah. David was a young shepherd boy playing music for King Saul when they met. *"As soon as David returned from killing the Philistine, Abner took him and brought him before Saul, with David still holding the Philistine's head...After David had finished talking with Saul, Jonathan became one in spirit with David, and he loved him as himself"* (1 Sam. 17:57, 18:1 NKJV). Jonathan was the king's son, already a great man of war. He was attracted to the strong faith of David; faith in the mighty God they both served as their common bond.

There were conflicting loyalties as well. Saul's jealousy of David provoked him to be on a lengthy mission to slay him. Jonathan put David's safety ahead of his father's desire to kill him, even if there was a high cost of doing so. When David replaced Saul to rule the nation as king, Jonathan was not jealous but supported him wholeheartedly. They stuck closer than brothers whatever life brought their way!

When God puts a lifetime friend in your life, your bond will not necessarily be because of your natural preferences. You may come from different cultural backgrounds or races, be of different class structures or educational levels and like David and Jonathan, there may be a significant age difference. But you will be one in spirit. This is a gift of God. I like what C.S. Lewis said about friendship. *"I have chosen you for one another. Friendship is not a reward for our discriminating and good taste in finding one another out. It is the instrument by which God reveals to each of us the beauty of others."* Indeed, the friend the Lord selects for me is a sterling treasure.

KEY OF NOT LOOKING BACK   During the time Aria and I were distant I had to learn not to dwell in the past; the memories, the hurt, the disappointments, my failures. I love what the Passion Translation Bible has to say about not looking at the former things: *"But forget all of that...It is nothing compared to what I have in store for you!"* (Is. 43:18). I made a choice to hand over my burden to the Lord and let Him resolve things in His way; yes, to forget all of that! It would require God's grace! My part was to thank Him for the coming answers and move forward.

Those days in Tucson that I suffered the loss of my home, my four-acre college campus and business, my reputation, and my husband, gave me plenty of reason for despair. Those things were gone. I couldn't change it, but focusing on my losses would have been my ruination. I could not afford to look back with bitterness, regret, or despair. I couldn't see the way out, but I thanked God anyway and kept my eyes on Him. Indeed, the Way He made for me was one that I never could have imagined... that one day I would be living right next door to my daughter, enjoying a full and healthy, restored relationship.

Dear Reader, whatever losses in life you may have had God is so much bigger. Praise Him for the answers and He will see you through. Look ahead with hope, not backward with regret. Your losses are surely a stepping stone to your destiny. The story is not over. God will work this into the texture of your life.

A story that drives this point home is that of MRS. LOT. The dramatic story of the biblical cities of Sodom and Gomorrah being destroyed by fire and brimstone because of their inhabitants' profound sin is recorded in Genesis 19. Although the Lord spared Lot and his wife by guiding them out of Sodom, Mrs. Lot could not resist looking back in disobedience. This resulted in her being smothered in a sarcophagus of immovable, rigid, lifeless salt...her shrine of unbelief!

The lure of looking back robbed her of her destiny. In her transition of leaving something behind, but not having yet reached her goal she succumbed to fear and insecurity, to sentimentality, to remember the '*good old days*'. She couldn't move past her pain. She couldn't say *"God has something better!"* Instead of putting her *foot-of-faith* in the Red Sea so God could part the waters and lead her to victory, she looked back, thus missing the blessing He intended for her.

I would say to Mrs. Lot, *"Keep moving! Run, walk, crawl if need be, but don't look back! Give up your excuses and rationalization! Embrace the transition period. It may require sacrifice, but God will make every provision for you. Just keep moving forward with your eyes on the Lord and His promises!"*

Looking back was a costly mistake! When God opens a door sometimes we, too, have excuses not to move forward. We might make the mistake Mrs. Lot did and allow sentimentality to rob us of our destiny. What might that cost? To move forward by faith or dwell in the old, familiar past is a choice with which we may be faced. What would be the line in the sand that could cause us to resist crossing over toward the next step in our destiny? Might I brush off God's nudging by saying, *"I am too old?"* or *"I could never move from here"* or *"I cannot afford it"* or *"I am too afraid of failure!"* Or any number of other excuses.

Paul writes, *"I do not consider myself yet to have taken hold of it, but one thing I do; forgetting that which is behind and straining toward what is ahead, I press on toward the goal to win the prize which God has called me heavenward in Christ Jesus!"* (Phil. 3:13-14).

I have read that in the game of baseball it is essential for the batter to keep his eye on the bases after hitting the ball and to run as fast as he can! The ball has been hit—-it was in the past! He cannot change how he did it. Keeping his eye on the ball rather than on his goal will at best slow him down, but more likely will stop his home run and scoring a victory! My victories have come as I kept my focus on Jesus, giving Him my failures and disappointments and just doing the very best I could in the present day He gave me. We can only reach our potential if we leave our past behind and forge forward. *"No one who puts his hand to the plow and looks back is fit for service in the kingdom of God"* (Luke 9:62).

KEY OF HOPE   A marvelous tool God has given each of us to help navigate hard times, losses, lengthy waiting periods and disappointments is hope. I don't know what I would have done without hope! Hope told me that no matter whatever I had lost there would be good things ahead. Hope has made me strong and courageous because I know God is for me and not against me. *"'I know the plans I have for you'", says the Lord, "Plans to prosper you and not to harm you, plans to give you hope and a future'..."* (Jer. 29:11). Rather than focus on unfulfilled dreams focus on the dream-giver instead. And dream BIG! Trading hopelessness for a BIG dream will change your outlook!

We must see through life's quandaries with the lens of hope. Hope is about knowing that there will be a good future. We don't hope for what we already have. Hope is about believing what God promised for our future. Hoping is the inner knowing that God has His best for you.

"Hurry up and wait" has been my life's mantra! I never could have survived the long waits I have endured without the blessed hope that things would improve! I have waited many years for some of my prayers to be answered. Some are still unanswered. But I know the answers are coming, just as many have already come! How do I know that? Because the Lord has proven Himself to me again and again to such an extent that I know that it is safe to HOPE! Now that I am in the golden years of my life, with wisdom acquired through life's experiences I still believe that the best is yet to come! That is hope! One must dream.

One must hope. One must have goals. As the old saying goes, *"Fail to plan (dream, hope, set goals), plan to fail!"*

The devil has lied to me many times to try to get me to give up hope. *Hope deferred not only makes one heart-sick or depressed* (Prov. 13:12) but will dilute or kill one's faith. Where there is faith there are miracles! No wonder the devil connives to discourage us! If he can get us to lose hope, we no longer will believe for our miracle. That's when the devil wins. Oh, dear Reader, keep on hoping. To give up hope is to QUIT! You cannot imagine the blessings the Lord has for you if you just keep hoping and trusting in Him. You may have to wait, but He never, ever, ever fails if you just believe. Keep hoping! And dream BIG!

Someone once said that hope is a walking dream! Maybe the reason you haven't yet seen your dream become a reality is that you haven't taken a step toward it. Bible heroes dared to go out on a limb, not letting their limitations and past failures keep them from their dreams. They may have had insecurities or lacked experience but they took a step of faith. For example, Esther had no prior experience delivering a nation. Debra never had been an army general before. Moses had no experience parting the Red Sea, nor had Peter ever walked on water.

I had never been an executive in a cosmetic company before; nor had I ever owned an interior design firm and showroom, an interior design school, a cultural tour business, or landscape design college before either. I never would have owned any of those without taking that first step. I would have missed many blessings had I not taken those first steps of faith.

We pray for a door to open, but too often when a door opens we lack the courage to step through it. How many of us have failed to discover our purpose because we feared failure? Behold the turtle. He only makes progress when he sticks his neck out.

KEY OF HAVING CHILDLIKE FAITH   The term *'Childlike faith'* is not found in the pages of the bible. But I do believe that the principle is often present throughout the scriptures. The Lord loves it when I become like a little child and just plain trust Him. Childlike faith is an innocent and confident trust in the goodness of God's plans for me. It is an approach in life in which one believes for the best without suspicion, cynicism, or fear. When I feed my faith my fear starves to death!

When the Word of God makes a promise, I may believe that God is well able to perform it, but my faith waivers as soon as I wonder, *"But will He do it for me?"*

Those times I have seen God move miraculously in my life were times that I just knew He would fulfill His Word. For example, the day I prayed for my friend Betty to be resurrected from death to life, there was no question about it! I was certain God would raise her up! His Word says we can pray for it and He will answer! And He did!

The day I needed to catch an international flight in Bangkok to get home to stall my house foreclosure, I needed to be on that flight! Although I got off to an unavoidable delay God had promised to meet all my needs! It was settled! He would give me a miracle of stretching one hour into two! There was no need to worry. He had said it and I believed it and I declared it! And He gave me my miracle!

God had planted a seed in my heart that I would be sent to England as an executive director of the American-based cosmetic company for whom I was working. It didn't matter that I was told it would be almost impossible to obtain the necessary working papers! I believed God would work out the details! I never doubted!

God's faithfulness would surely prevail by providing that motorcycle helmet for my little boy. He knew how essential it would be for young Patrick to witness God the Father's love and generosity toward him! I just knew He would do it!

In all those instances I knew without a doubt that my God heard me and would answer. I had childlike faith. I wish I could say that every time I have prayed my faith was one hundred percent utter childlike belief and trust. Although there have been many times my faith has wavered, walking in childlike faith can become a lifestyle; a mind-set. Just like anything else in which we want to become proficient, it requires practice. I couldn't become a concert pianist without practice.

What is it about a child that our faith needs to emulate? A child is innocent and pure-hearted. He or she looks to his natural father with undivided complete trust to meet every need. If I want to understand how to trust God I just remember how my children completely trusted me without question for their needs to be met. Oh! Might I maintain that pure-hearted innocence of a child. *"Create in me a pure heart, O God, and renew a steadfast spirit within me!"* (Ps. 51:10).

A child is equipped with natural wonder and awe; that wide-eyed amazing wonder at God's creation. No matter how wise or sophisticated I become, or how much I learn in life, may I never lose the simple faith, trust, and pure heart of a child!

THE KEY OF KNOWING THAT GOD LOVES ME:

This book has now come full circle. In the first chapter I wrote of my Damascus Road experience; the powerful encounter I had many years ago of tasting the immensity of God's love for me. That Love has carried me through many trials, disappointments, and testings as well as glorious victories, too. Through it all I have never doubted that He loved me. One touch of God's love was all I needed for a lifetime of confidence in Him. Because I am certain of His amazing love for me I have a rock-solid confidence that is unshakable. That confidence has enabled me to take risks and to step outside of the bounds of normal insecurity. That is because my confidence is really God-confidence rather than self-confidence or self-consciousness. What a difference!

The greatest tool in my life's arsenal has been knowing that He is for me and not against me, that He loves me with an everlasting love and will never leave me nor forsake me. His love for me is the foundation of my life. May I never lose sight of the depth of His marvelous love for me!

He loves you like that, too. Believe it and you will never be the same. Your confidence will soar. If God is for you who can be against you?

Because I know that He loves me perfectly and unconditionally I know He wants me to love others in my life, too. The challenge of life is to love as Jesus loves. I want to be so saturated with God's love that it just spills out of me onto those I encounter.

God's Word says that He thought of us in the beginning. He created mankind before He ever manifested man and woman on earth. Long before I was manifested or born in time on earth, He had a destiny and a design for me. I have come to understand that as I walk in that destiny He is glorified. As I was deeply engrossed in playing a demanding Beethoven piano sonata recently I had a revelation of the Lord smiling at me, *"My child, I created you to be musical. You were born with a seed of musical talent. When I see you have developed it and now bring music into the world, I am glorified."* I realized that when I exercise my talents and uniqueness He is glorified through me. I can walk in such freedom by being who He created me to be, not by trying to be someone else that I may admire. For many years I didn't play much classical music believing it only blessed the Lord if I played *'Christian music'.* That was a legalistic religious mind-set. Whatever I play to the glory of God brings Him joy. So I play for Him...Beethoven, Chopin, Bach, Schumann, Scriabin, Brahams and many other composers as well as my beloved Christian praise and worship music. I am free and He is glorified!

It is time for all of us to bring glory to God on earth by being the unique person He created us to be; to be a receptor of His love and allow that love to spill out to others. This is what will transform our lives, our culture, our world.

To add to those keys I have just shared with you, I am closing this book with Declarations that you may speak out loud over your life any time you like. Many of the victories in my life have been a result of declaring and decreeing God's Word. These Declarations are my gift to you to bring power and victory to your life, too! They are powerful and will transform your life if you just believe and decree them. The demons in the atmosphere will flee when they hear the truth of the Word! Angels are dispatched to accomplish miracles in your life when they *"hearken"* to the *"VOICE of His Word"*! They must not only hear it but the word *"hearken"* implies action. They await their assignments by keenly listening or *"hearkening"* for the Word of God to be dispatched! *"Bless the Lord, you His angels, who excel in strength, who do His bidding, hearkening to the VOICE of His Word"* (Ps. 103:20 KJV).

I impart abundant blessings and God's favor to spill out over your life that you might bring God's glory to earth and impact all those whose lives you touch!

DAILY PERSONAL DECLARATIONS

I DECLARE God's blessings will chase me down and overtake me with sudden increase and favor! God will open up supernatural doors for me. I declare I have the grace I need for today. I am full of power, strength, and determination. Nothing I face will be too much for me. I will overcome every obstacle, outlast every challenge, and come through every difficulty.

I DECLARE everything that doesn't line up with God's vision for my life is subject to change. Sickness, trouble, lack, and mediocrity are not permanent. I will not be moved by what I see but by what I know. I am a victor and never a victim. I will become all God has created me to be.

I DECLARE I will experience God's faithfulness. I will not worry, doubt or fear! I will trust Him knowing that He will not fail me. I am thankful for who God is in my life. I will not take for granted the people, opportunities, and favor He has given me. I will look at what is right and not what is wrong. I will thank Him for what I have and not complain about what I don't have. Each day as a gift from God. My heart will overflow with praise and gratitude for His goodness.

I DECLARE a legacy of faith over my life. I declare that I will store up blessings for future generations. My life is marked by excellence. God has a Master Plan for my life. He is directing my steps. He will work out every detail to my advantage. In His perfect timing, everything will work out just right. My destiny will not be stopped by people, disappointments, or adversities. I will see Eph. 3:20 *"exceedingly, abundantly, above and beyond favor and increase"* in my life. I will give birth to every promise God put in my heart and will become everything God created me to be.

I DECLARE I have a sound mind filled with good thoughts, not thoughts of defeat or failure. I am well able, anointed, equipped, and empowered by the Holy Spirit. My thoughts are guided by God's Word every day. No obstacle can defeat me because My mind is programmed for victory.

I DECLARE I am filled with wisdom. I make good choices. I have clear direction. I am blessed with creativity, good ideas, courage, and ability. I am blessed with good health, a good family, good friends, and a long life. I am blessed with promotion, success, an obedient heart, and a positive outlook. Whatever I put my hands to will prosper and succeed. I will be blessed in the city, and the field. I will be blessed when I go in and when I go out. I will lend and not borrow and I will be above and not beneath.

I DECLARE I will speak only positive words of faith and victory over myself, my family, and my future. I will not use my words to describe my situation. I will use my words to change my situation. I will call in favor, good breaks, healing, and restoration. I will not talk to God about how big my problems are; I will talk to my problems about how big my God is! I will not just survive, I will thrive! I will prosper despite every difficulty that may come my way. Every setback is a set-up for a comeback. God is working all things together for good in my life.

I DECLARE that every bondage and limitation is being broken off of me. Every negative word and curse that has ever been spoken over me is broken in the name of Jesus. I declare that the negative things that have been in my family even for generations will no longer have any effect on me. I believe that in the spiritual realm things have been set into motion. Curses have been broken and blessings are on their way.

I DECLARE I am special and extraordinary. I have been custom-made! I am one of a kind. I am His Masterpiece, His prized possession. I will keep my head held high knowing I am a child of the Most High God, made in His very image. It is not too late to accomplish everything that God has placed in my heart. This is my moment; my time to shine.

BECOMING A CHILD OF GOD

1. Repent of your past sins and recognize your need for a Savior. *("All have sinned and fall short of the glory of God"* (Rom. 3:23).

2. Realize that Jesus is the only way to God. *(I am the Way, the Truth, and the Life. No one comes to the Father but by me"* (John 14:6).

3. Invite Jesus to come into your heart to reside forever. *("I stand at the door and knock. If any man hears my voice and opens the door I will come into him and sup with him and he with me"* (Rev. 3:20).

4. Thank Him and begin an eternal relationship with Him. Find a church to attend that preaches the Word of God and begin to read the Bible.

DISCLAIMER

This book was written based on the truth as I remember it to have been. Some names or details have been changed to protect the privacy of those about whom I have written.

CPSIA information can be obtained
at www.ICGtesting.com
Printed in the USA
LVHW050410040721
691861LV00007B/326